Understanding God's Love and Life's Polarities

by Emmitt J. Nelson

Published by Nelson Consulting, Inc.

ISBN 0-9664896-9-1

Manufactured in the United States of America

First Edition

INTRODUCTION

Pope Benedict was recently quoted as saying as he addressed the "intelligent design of the universe" issue now before the public in Christian nations that the basic reason God created the universe and the world we live upon is "love."

Based on this premise, pure logic argues that it is through creation that God's love is to be revealed, shared and practiced by His "likeness," man. In my opinion the Bible, in the whole, teaches this truth very clearly.

My purpose in composing this narrative is to show support for this view through the use of logic that is available to all thinking beings. This logic is, of course, apparent to all but especially apparent to one who has accepted God's total plan and is a member of the Family of God, through belief in His Son Jesus Christ.

Such a relationship with God enlightens the "....eyes of the heart...." as mentioned in Ephesians 1:17-18

> 17 I keep asking that the God of our Lord Jesus Christ, the glorious Father, may give you the Spirit of wisdom and revelation, so that you may know him better.
> 18 I pray also that the eyes of your heart may be enlightened in order that you may know the hope to which he has called you, the riches of his glorious inheritance in the saints, NIV

God's Love and Life's Polarities

Life as we know it is filled with contrasts. Physicists along with other professions would name these contrasts with the term "polarities." The word "polarity" is a form of the root word "Polar." Polar as defined by Webster is as follows:

Polar – 1. a. of, relating to, or near the North or South Pole. b. coming from the region near the North or South Pole.
2. of a pole or poles.
3. having polarity.
4. <u>opposite in character, nature, direction etc.</u>
5. central and guiding, like the earth's pole or the polestar.

When I use the term polarity as I am applying it by the definition number 4 above; <u>opposite in character, nature, direction, etc.</u>

I am quite sure as I engage in this effort that in the pages below I have omitted a number of rather germane Bible scriptures that support my thesis and for that I am remorseful. I excuse this omission in my work by observing that, were one to work a lifetime one would never completely exhaust the Bible as a resource to prove the point that God created for love.

I believe that God, through His revealed nature definitively proves the ultimate meaning of the word "logical."

I will delve into the Logic of God and assist the reader in gaining understanding of and about God's Love and also to encourage the reader to think of God not only from a spiritual perspective but also in an applied logical manner.

Even as I take on the task of exploring this vast and diverse subject please be assured that I am deeply aware of my meager offerings as I attempt to describe the nature of God recalling Isaiah 55:8-9.

> 8 "For My thoughts are not your thoughts, nor are
> your ways My ways," declares the LORD. 9 "For as
> the heavens are higher than the earth, so are My
> ways higher than your ways and My thoughts than
> your thoughts."

However remember 1 Cor 2:10-13 that does speak of a spiritual empowerment coming through the Holy Spirit that can enlighten man with spiritual words.

> 10 For to us God revealed them through the Spirit; for
> the Spirit searches all things, even the depths of God.
> 11 For who among men knows the thoughts of a man
> except the spirit of the man which is in him? Even so
> the thoughts of God no one knows except the Spirit of
> God. 12 Now we have received, not the spirit of the
> world, but the Spirit who is from God, so that we may
> know the things freely given to us by God, 13 which
> things we also speak, not in words taught by human
> wisdom, but in those taught by the Spirit, combining
> spiritual thoughts with spiritual words. NASU

All the scripture appearing in this work are extracted from PC Study BibleTM Version 2, CD ROM edition sold by BIBLESOFT© of Seattle, Washington.

TABLE OF CONTENTS

Chapters

CHAPTER 1

We Ask, "Why?"

Why, in the Biblical account of the Garden of Eden, would an all wise creating God allow the presence of an evil force like the Serpent?

Would you be surprised if I said this fact is one of the first evidences in the Bible of the grand extent of "God's Love" for His creation man?

You then might ask; "Where do you get this idea; what kind of a God would allow the existence of evil to show His love?"

To answer this we must analyze creation. Doing so one finds that all creation is filled with polarities, contrasts, or opposites.

Let's look at the Bible at the story of creation as recorded by Moses – in the beginning God created. God created "something." Before that there was "nothing."

> Gen 1:1 In the beginning God created the Heavens and the Earth.

Then we see the writer of Hebrews from 2000 years ago records a concept that even today has become the fodder of scientists who postulate the creation of the earth, yes even the universe occurred at the time of a "big bang."

> Heb 11:1-3
> 11:1 Now faith is being sure of what we hope for and certain of what we do not see. 2 This is what the ancients were commended for.
> 3 By faith we understand that the universe was formed at God's command, so <u>that what is seen was not made out of what was visible.</u> NIV

It is the last 12 words of the above verse that tells all and aligns with current astronomical thought that what we have for a universe began in an instant in time in the distant past and originated from a "singularity point;" a astronomical word that means "from nothing."

<u>Polarities Introduced</u>

Above we have the first polarity; there was nothing then there was something. Contained in that something we see early evidence of something human life could not exist without – water. And water is made of two elements that are critical to the final life on earth product; hydrogen and oxygen.

Next, we see the second polarity created; light versus darkness.

> Gen 1:2. Now the earth was formless and empty, darkness was over the surface of the deep, and the Spirit of God was hovering over the waters
> 3 And God said, "Let there be light," and there was light.
> 4 God saw that the light was good, and he separated the light from the darkness. NIV

Next, we see the third polarity; wet vs. dry.

> Gen 1:9 And God said, "Let the water under the sky be gathered to one place, and let dry ground appear." NIV

Next, we see the fourth polarity; barren vs. vegetation.

> Gen 1:11 Then God said, "Let the land produce vegetation: seed-bearing plants and trees on the land that bear fruit with seed in it, according to their various kinds." NIV

Next, we see the fifth polarity; no life vs. living creatures.

> Gen 1:20 And God said, "Let the water teem with living creatures, and let birds fly above the earth across the expanse of the sky." NIV

Next, we see the sixth polarity; male and female.

> Gen 1:27 So God created man in his own image, in the image of God he created him; male and female he created them. NIV

Have you ever wondered why the wings and strength of birds are equally matched to the density of air with the wing size and muscular power of the birds that enable bird flight? Were the air less dense birds as they are could not fly. What if the air was only 30% as dense as it is; could we live in such an environment? Perhaps; but several things would be drastically different; either the percentage oxygen in the air would have to be much greater or our lungs would have to be much bigger or we would have to be much smaller. I cover this thought to give the reader pause to consider we are indeed living on an earth where everything is balanced.

Notice how it was all perfectly balanced in the creation process for things to be as they are. There are literally thousands of critical factors prevalent on earth for human life to exist here; so much so that learned scientists conclude there had to be "intelligent design.'

The final polarity mentioned in Genesis thus created by God was:

> Gen 2:1 Thus the heavens and the earth were completed in all their vast array.
> 2 By the seventh day God had finished the work he had been doing; so on the seventh day he rested from all his work.
> 3 And God blessed the seventh day and made it holy, because on it he rested from all the work of creating that he had done.
> 4 This is the account of the heavens and the earth when they were created. NIV

The seventh polarity was - God recognized "rest;" the opposite of his creative "work."

Looked at in this way, one can see God, in fact, created (and Moses mentions in Genesis) seven basic, yet simple, polarities in the seven days. I do not consider this concept as a mind bending revelation. Obviously there were many additional polarities created. Thus to understand creation and the created world we must understand the absolute necessity for the existence of "polarities!"

CHAPTER 2

God's Created Polarities

The above seven polarities are not, by far, the only opposites created, for there are many if one stops to analyze the result of God's creation activity.

God's basic seven.

Something vs. Nothing
Light vs. Dark
Wet vs. Dry
Barren vs. Vegetation
No Creature life vs. Creature Life
Man – Male and Female
Work vs. Rest

A look at a few additional polarity concepts reveals the following:

Positive vs. Negative
North Pole vs. South Pole
East vs. West

The earth is a magnetic body joined by gravity within our solar system to the planet we call the Sun. The earth moves through space at a tremendous velocity that we are not aware of as it circles the Sun. Further our planetary system is also moving through space in conjunction with the Milky Way Galaxy at something like 200 miles per second. In the time it takes to say the word "velocity" you will have traveled 200 miles through space as a part of our Galaxy.

We could name this polarity "Moving versus Stopped."

We can stop in relation to another object on earth but we can never stop as a part of our moving planet.

To name more I offer the following list of commonly known yet simple polarities:

Sweet vs. Sour
Hard vs. Soft
Bland vs. Salty
White vs. Black
Cold vs. Hot
On vs. Off
Soiled vs. Clean
High vs. Low
Focused vs. Blurred
Sight vs. Blind
Open vs. Closed
Weight/Gravity vs. Weightless
Up vs. Down
Hungry vs. Well Fed

Lean vs. Fat
Well vs. Sick

Then as we look at our existence in this created world we also have what I term the moral polarities –

Love vs. Hate
Good versus Evil
Sinless versus Sinful

As one can see, the above three are inter-related as we go through our everyday lives. This brings us back to the question of "Why did God create and why did an all knowing God allow evil to be a part of His creation?"

> *The answer, I believe is – To allow the fullness of God's great love to be demonstrated in the hearts of men!*

Following is the supporting logic and upon examination we find the same discourse also explains the logic behind the enormity of God's love. Statement of fact; "Love is a condition of the heart and mind."

Logical Premise: For a condition to exist the potential for the opposite condition must also exist.

The opposite of "moving" is "stopped."

The opposite of "floating" is "sinking."

The opposite of "a smile is a frown."

Try the following challenges.

Try if you will to define "warmth" without using the concept of something being "colder," or the absence of warmth.

Try to define "barren" without the concept of "vegetative growth."

Try to define "wet" without the concept of something being "dry."

As we go through life we all experience sickness, thus try to explain sickness without the concept of being and feeling well. Therefore as one can see, to experience or to define "love," a contrast must exist as well. This contrasting opposite of God's Love is "evil or the Serpent or Satan" or as an emotion "hate."

So, if the mere definition of love requires the use of an opposite concept, it follows that for "love" to be demonstrated by Man in action the option must therefore exist for Man to act with "hate or evil." Given this polarity, and knowing God seeks our utmost devotion and love, think about the following:

The greater the freedom we have to be or do evil, the greater is the emotional value to God when we truly seek God "with all our heart" and He feels the grandeur of our unfettered love for Him; and also as this occurs the greater His reward to us in "spiritual well being" as we faithfully serve Him.

CHAPTER 3

Eden Created

God's Gift to Man; a Perfect Place to Live; The Garden of Eden

The creation story in Genesis comes in two chapters, with Chapter 2, verses 4-25 overlaid onto Chapter 1. For instance Chapter 2 verse 7 coincides with Chapter 1 verse 27. The overlay is not verse by verse but subject oriented. Chapter 1 is chronological, Chapter 2 is not.

> Genesis 2:7-8
> 7: Then the Lord God formed man of the dust from the ground, and breathed into his nostrils the breath of life, and man became a living being.
> 8: And the Lord God planted a garden toward the east in Eden; and there He placed the man He had formed.

This garden was the place many ask questions about when they ask why God allows sickness and tragedy. The answer is He allowed His created man to choose his future conditions and our patriarch, Adam, made a bad choice.

As proof of God's intentions we see Genesis 1:28 chartering Adam to "be fruitful and multiply and fill the earth and subdue it." Being fruitful and multiplying it seems would be about procreation of the human population, but when we see the words "subdue it" to me this implies God is also telling man to be inventive, find ways to utilize the earth as a natural resource. This tells me God is pro-technology and is pleased when man finds some new technical advance that makes life easier.

When God expelled man from the Garden I do not feel this "subdue it" challenge to man was in any way altered, but obviously man's challenge was made more difficult thus making these technological advances even harder.

Also to properly "subdue the earth" to me means God is pro-education and pro-self improvement.

> Genesis 1:27-29
> 27: And God created man in His own image, in the image of God He created him, male and female He created them.
> 28: And God blessed them; and God said to them, "Be fruitful and multiply and fill the earth and subdue it; and rule over the fish of the sea and over the birds of the sky and over ever living thing that moves on the earth.
> 29: Then God said, "Behold, I have given you every plant yielding seed that is on the surface of all the

earth, and every tree which has fruit yielding seed, it shall be food for you.

I have a question here. If God prescribed food for the first physically perfect man and woman He created and that food was of the "plants yielding seed and every tree whose fruit yield seed" might those things be the best diet for us today?

The First Man Fails to Live by God's Instructions

Later in Chapter 6 of Genesis God introduces a covenant relationship between God and man. However the word "covenant" between God and Adam is not mentioned in Genesis. God did however issue a commandment and this commandment can be considered in fact a covenant. If Adam would abide by the commandment then Adam's blessings would be great.

Gen 2:15-17
15 The LORD God took the man and put him in the Garden of Eden to work it and take care of it. 16 And the LORD God commanded the man, "You are free to eat from any tree in the garden; 17 but you must not eat from the tree of the knowledge of good and evil, for when you eat of it you will surely die." NIV

As all know Adam's sin was one of disobedience, but the act was not called "sin" in the Genesis account though it clearly was. Genesis Chapter 3 tells the story of Adam's disobeying God's first "commandment." of not eating from the tree of "knowledge of good and evil."

Let's think about the commandment for a moment. Though God had to allow evil as the opposite polarity of love, He nonetheless attempted to protect man from this knowledge of evil. Were Adam to have obeyed God, rather than failed, one can only wonder what the world would be like today.

One could readily conclude it might be something like heaven. Or one could conclude a place where all we would do would be to eat, enjoy life with Eve and God would provide everything else.

Logic suggests otherwise; it is hard to imagine and not logical in my mind for God create man to leave us, even in a Garden, without a daily physical and mental challenge. "Take care of it" (the Garden of Eden) was man's first challenge.

So if you want to go on an imaginary journey, mentally delve into the notion that, were we as a human race to not know evil, the world is a drastically different place with totally different operational norms than now. But, it is just a "what if" for man failed to obey and we have "this." You can define "this" as world conditions caused by our forebears and sustained by us even as some of us attempt to alter them for the better as others attempt to send us into further moral decay.

CHAPTER 4

Conflict in the First Family

Adam's Curse

Adam and Eve were expelled from the Garden of Eden for breaking God's commandment and all mankind were given a curse as punishment.

After the failure of Adam and Eve to obey God; and after they were driven out of the Garden of Eden, "sin" continued to plague their family as their first born son killed their second born son.

Sin Named and Confirmed by God

While the sin of Adam and Eve was clearly that, the disobedience was not called "sin" in the Genesis account. It was later, on the occasion of Cain killing Able that the word "sin" is introduced by God when he verbally chastised Cain for not accepting God's refusal of Cain's offering from his flocks. In this rebuke, it is implied there was something wrong with Cain's attitude about the offering.

> Gen 4:2 Now Abel kept flocks, and Cain worked the soil. 3 In the course of time Cain brought some of the fruits of the soil as an offering to the LORD.
> 4 But Abel brought fat portions from some of the firstborn of his flock. The LORD looked with favor on Abel and his offering,
> 5 but on Cain and his offering he did not look with favor. So Cain was very angry, and his face was downcast.
> 6 Then the LORD said to Cain, "Why are you angry? Why is your face downcast?
> 7 If you do what is right, will you not be accepted? But if you do not do what is right, sin is crouching at your door; it desires to have you, but you must master it." NIV

So what was Cain's problem? I do not believe it was the offering per se' but something more sinister.

It may be found in the words "In the course of time... Cain brought some of the fruits of the soil...." The words "In the course of time" restated means, "when Cain got around to it" implying that Cain's offering was not from the first crop but came later; not necessarily the "best" nor the "first fruits." Whereas, Able brought the "fat of the first born" and God was pleased. That type of offering later was exactly, with a few modifications what God instructed the Israelites to bring to the Alter of Sacrifice.

An attitude analysis readily yields the recognition that Cain's offering was not a first priority, thus it came from a lax and flawed attitude. In any case God was not pleased and Cain grew "very angry."

And God asked Cain; "Why are you angry?"

Focus on verses 7 for Cain's problem.

> Vs 7 "If you do what is right, will you not be accepted?" But if you do not do what is right, sin is crouching at your door; it desires you, but you must master it."

Sin was here identified by God as "...not doing what is right..." in one's relationship with God. In Cain's case it was a matter of honoring God with timely given first fruits as opposed to "bringing an offering in the course of time.'" If God instructs and we fail to follow, that failure defines sin.

As we see Cain was immediately angry with God when God did not accept his offering. Cain apparently did not seek the reason for God's refusal; his anger at being rejected was immediate, total and became a barrier to his relationship with God. There was apparently no thought on Cain's part that he might have a greater problem. Cain obviously needed an attitude adjustment. Also note that God did not call Cain's "anger" Cain's sin.

The Bible allows anger, but it demands that such anger be righteous anger. In the case of Cain It is not the anger that is the root sin. As with Cain anger is often the result of sin in our heart, mind and soul.

Anger comes often out of an attitude of "the pride of life." Anger comes when internally we take issue with a circumstance or situation. We take issue because of a perception we have of some value we hold being violated. Sometimes the anger is righteous anger (perhaps at times a self-righteous anger) and at other times anger comes out of a misapplication of our personal values. Scripture on anger follows:

> Eph 4:26-27
> 6 "In your anger do not sin": Do not let the sun go
> down while you are still angry, 27 and do not give the
> devil a foothold. NIV

> James 1:19-20
> 19 My dear brothers, take note of this: Everyone should
> be quick to listen, slow to speak and slow to become
> angry, 20 for man's anger does not bring about the
> righteous life that God desires. NIV

Cain's killing of Abel affected God's plan for man and altered forever the future of mankind. Let's look at Adams's lineage for perspective.

CHAPTER 5

Adam's Lineage

One thing we know Adam did well. He and his offspring did a good job of "multiplying." This is evidenced when right in the middle of the story of Creation; Genesis Chapter 5 is inserted where we are given the lineage of Adam in 32 verses covering some 1600 years of the expansion of the human race upon the earth from Adam to Noah.

Experts have estimated that the human population at the time Adam died at about 150,000. Now that's a big family!

The Bible records Adam dieing at the age of 930. If one does a "lineage look-back" in Chapter 5 from before Adam died there were nine generations of male family members living with their offspring at the time of Adam's death. It is interesting that in the lineage we see that Seth was born when Adam was 130. We do not know the earlier age of Adam when Cain or Able was born.

Checking out my "nine generations living claim" we see the following from analyzing Seth's descendants:
1- God Created Adam – died in 930 AAC (AAC = After Adam Created)

Adam begat – Abel and Cain then Seth -

2 - Seth born in 130AAC – dies in 937 AAC

Seth begat -

3 - Enosh born in 235 AAC – died in 1140 AAC

Enosh begat -

4 - Kenan born in 325AAC – died in 1235 AAC

Kenan begat -

5 - Mahalalel born in 395AAC – died in 1290 AAC

Mahalalel begat -

6 - Jared born in 460AAC – died in 1422 AAC

Jared begat -

7 - Enoch born in 622AAC – taken by God in 987 AAC

The Bible says Enoch walked with God 300 years after Methusela was born beginning when Enoch was 65 until he was 365 years of age in 987 AAC.

For clarity Cain's first son was also named Enoch and could have been born about the same time as Seth.

Enoch of Jared begat -

8 - Methusela born in 687AAC – died in 1656 AAC (1656 AAC is the year the flood began)

Methusela begat –

9 - Lamech born in 874 AAC – died in1651 AAC

Lamech, the eighth descendent was born in 874 and Adam dies in 930 AAC so for 57 years there were nine generations of Adam's line living. Enoch was taken 57 years later.

The Bible says Enoch was "taken up" by God in 987 AAC.

The above Lamech was in Seth's lineage.

Please note there was also an Enoch and a Lamech in Cain's lineage, the latter being a great, great, great grandson of Cain and the first to marry two women. See Genesis Chapter 4:19.

Also note that Adam dies in 930 AAC (Enoch was taken in 987AAC) during this time frame, some 56 years after Lamech was born and 126 years before Noah was born. Thus the nine generations.

Lamech of Seth's lineage begat -
10. Noah born in 1056 AAC – died in 2006 AAC

The flood came in Noah's 600th year thus in the year 1656 AAC; the same year Methusela died at age 969. Question: The Bible states only that he died in that year; so was he killed by the flood? It is and interesting question that has no answer.

Noah begat -
11. Shem, Ham, Japheth born in 1556 AAC.

In Genesis Chapter 5 verse 32 we see in Noah's 500th year the three sons were born to him. As an interesting aside; I have never heard that Shem, Ham, and Japheth were triplets but one could conclude such.

If not triplets and if all three were born in Noah's 500th year then considering a 350-360 day year and 270 day human gestation period it is possible for the three to have been a set of twins with an older or younger brother, all born in the 12 month period of Noah's 500th year.

> Gen 5:32 And Noah was five hundred years old, and became the father of Shem, Ham, and Japheth.

Females for Men to Marry

Note - While we know our matriarch Eve's name we do not know how long Eve lived but we do know she lived long enough to bear "...other sons and daughters..." to Adam.

Note - Where Seth and Cain obtained their wives, unless they married their sisters we have no clue. Or as some might consider, since God created Eve, what was to keep God from creating a few more females if He so chose? But on the quite logical subject of marrying sisters we see in Gen 5:4 that after Seth was born Adam fathered "other sons and daughters."

> Gen 5:4 After Seth was born, Adam lived 800 years and had other sons and daughters. NIV

Not only this but Seth was all of 105 years old before his son Enosh was born; thus allowing plenty of time for a goodly number of sisters to have been born and come of marrying age prior to Enosh's mother giving birth.

> Gen 5:6
> 6 When Seth had lived 105 years, he became the father of Enosh. NIV

Having said all the above I readily admit, we in fact simply do not know where Cain's and Seth's wife originated but one does not have to be very original to postulate they married their sisters. They were all perfect in biological form anyway, having not been of the human race long enough to acquire the negative hereditary traits (DNA?) caused by siblings marrying that we humans acquired in later centuries.

Men Followed After God

As we saw above in the last statement in the 4th Chapter of Genesis the good news; "...then men began to call upon the name of Jehovah...."

Thus for some extended number of years then, it was common for men to call upon God. Just how long was this "call upon God period?" I personally conjecture that this period where "man sought God" referenced in Genesis 4:26 was likely for about 700 hundred years. (Adam was 235 when Enosh was born and died at age 930, a period of 694 years.)

I offer this "700 years" idea since one can easily imagine, Adam, the patriarch being present coaching, urging and telling and retelling his experience in the Garden of Eden and why his offspring should worship and honor God.

Then we also find that until somewhere around the mid 600's, Enoch, 622 – 987 AAC (who the Bible says "walked with God") was present to assist Adam if we logically assume this "walking with God" was of a stalwart spiritual nature. Of all the early descendents of Adam, Enoch is the only one identified as "walking with God."

One can readily see until Adam's death in 930 AAC, mankind had the witness of the original "God created" family patriarch Adam who had walked in the Garden with God. I believe it is highly plausible to assume that Adam was always reminding his family of the greatness of God and reminding them that, in fact, God was the family's all powerful creating God and to honor Him in all things.

Do you think just because Cain killed Able that Adam never again communicated with Cain's family? I think not; I would think that just as Adam likely did for Seth's descendants, Adam also did for Cain's descendant's as always urging them to follow God doing this for as long as Adam lived.

We must conclude, if this postulation is true and there is every reason to believe accordingly, that Adam with likely assistance from Enoch enjoyed a modicum of success for a long period as he admonished his family to follow God and to honor Him. To support this, note that the scripture does not single out Seth's lineage as "walking with God" rather used the word "men" implying all men.

Bad News

In contrast to Genesis 4:26 where it is stated "...men began to call upon the name of Jehovah...," we find that after Adam died (930 AAC) and Enoch was taken up by God (987 AAC) and as man populated the Earth, morals deteriorated and God's influence decreased and man's wickedness became great.

We see this early in verse 5 of the fifth chapter of Genesis just thirty five verses after Genesis 4:26.

> Gen 6:5 The LORD saw how great man's wickedness on the earth had become, and that every inclination of the thoughts of his heart was only evil all the time.
> 6 The LORD was grieved that he had made man on the earth, and his heart was filled with pain.
> 7 So the LORD said, "I will wipe mankind, whom I have created, from the face of the earth--men and animals, and creatures that move along the ground, and birds of the air--for I am grieved that I have made them."

So here is a puzzle; we find God "grieved" He had created at all. By implication it is hard to avoid the notion that God was not only sorry, but again by implication, He perhaps did not know from the beginning that His creation would turn out so badly; or perhaps He did not anticipate that man would be so enticed by the pleasures brought about by misuse of the carnal mind and body in striving after evil.

In other words the Serpent was winning the minds and hearts of man. Such "God did not know" logic flies in the face of defining God as "all knowing, all powerful, all seeing, all present God, I AM THAT I AM." Even so, some conclude from the Genesis verbiage that it seems God, the all knowing Creator, did not foresee that mankind would fall so thoroughly to the wily nature of the evil one.

Personally, I believe God knew this all along but was nonetheless discouraged when it happened. This should be instructive to us. For since this was God's first (as far as we know) time to create humans, even knowing there would be the opportunity to sin, God nonetheless, was so offended when he saw what evil the heart of man was capable of, he repented that He had made man to begin with.

What was missing?

8 But Noah found favor in the eyes of the LORD.

Might man's missing life style ingredient been the lack of an emphasis on "heart love" toward God?

There is one thing that is very instructive about this creation history; that is that God will tolerate sin for a time but not forever. God tolerated man in his sin for some ~600 years (Adam died at age 930 AAC) before God said "no more" and called on Noah to build the Arc. Noah was 500 years old when God called him in ~year 1556 AAC. Then it took 100 years for Noah to construct the Ark and thus it was in

Noah's 600th year that the flood occurred. So God tolerated sin for as much a 726 years prior to the flood. (1656 – 930 = 726)

From the words in Genesis 6, one can conclude that even though God was discouraged at the sinfulness of man, nonetheless He continued to work out man's future salvation. God knew in advance, that in the mind of His creation man, without some form of specific moral guidance, the lure of selfish carnal fulfillment overpowers any bent of man to seek God.

From this one can conclude God determined that in order for man to have a chance of placing his trust in God for a lifetime that man would need more specific life style guidance along with a means of reconciliation to an all righteous God.

CHAPTER 6

God's Covenants (of love) with Man

Now that I have mentioned God's covenants with Adam and Noah let's deal with God's continuation of those covenants with man. We learn from the Bible that there are two basic and primary Covenants given by God to His creation man.

These are portrayed in the Old Testament (the first Covenant) and in the New Testament (the second or new Covenant). In reading the scripture I find what I feel are 6 re-statements of the first Covenant with the 8th being the final advent of the second covenant.

Though "covenant as a word" is not used in the Genesis account of Adam it is used by Hosea in describing God's relationship with Adam.

> Hosea 6:7
> 7 Like Adam, they have broken the covenant - they were unfaithful to me there. NIV

The first covenant is;

1. with Adam, the Garden Covenant

The 6 re-statements:

2. With Noah, The first re-statement.
3. With Abram, The second re-statement.
4. With Isaac, The third re-statement.
5. With Jacob/Israel, The fourth re-statement.
6. With Israelites through Moses, The fifth re-statement.
7. With David through Nathan the Prophet, the sixth re-statement.

The Salvation Covenant:

8. with all mankind through Jesus Christ.

After Adam, each succeeding covenant re-statement, I believe, marked a continuation of the relationship until the New Testament covenant when, I believe, God radically changed His relationship with man.

The immediate question of course is "how did it change?"

The relationship changed from one where man provided the sin offering to one where God provided the sin offering for all time and for all peoples. I am not saying God changed. God is God and the great "I AM" therefore does not change; but His relationship to man changed. The Bible even foretells of this change in

> Jer 31:33
> 33 "This is the covenant I will make with the house of Israel after that time," declares the LORD. "I will put my

law in their minds and write it on their hearts. I will be their God, and they will be my people. NIV

Covenant Re-statements

The first Covenant re-statement with Noah was a promise from God to preserve the human race.

While recognizing all the covenants were all about love, the next re-statements were with Abram, Isaac, and Jacob and were lead-in to the Covenant of the Ten Commandments which was the first "so stated covenant of 'Love.'"

> Deut 7:8 But it was because the LORD loved you and kept the oath he swore to your forefathers that he brought you out with a mighty hand and redeemed you from the land of slavery, from the power of Pharaoh king of Egypt.
> 9 Know therefore that the LORD your God is God; he is the faithful God, keeping his covenant of love to a thousand generations of those who love him and keep his commands. NIV

The two principal covenants and all the re-statements were made to allow God, over time, to build a relationship with a race of people so He could relate with and to all sinful men and thus provide the medium for His ultimate reconciliation of man to Himself through His love expressed through His only Son, Jesus Christ.

Love is Introduced by God

Then in Exodus 20:1-17; God gives the people the 10 Commandments; the Moses Covenant. In these God uses the "love" word the first time; saying He will "show love to a thousand generations.

> Ex 20:4-6
> Thou shall not make for yourself an idol in the form of anything in heaven above or on the earth beneath or in the waters below. 5 You shall not bow down to them or worship them; for I, the LORD your God, am a jealous God, punishing the children for the sin of the fathers to the third and fourth generation of those who hate me, 6 but showing love to a thousand [generations] of those who love me and keep my commandments. NIV

Moses wrote the covenant down and read it to the people. Exodus 24:4&7.

> G.24:4 And Moses wrote down all the words of the Lord. Then he arose early in the morning, and built an Alter at the foot of the mountain with twelve pillars for the tribes of Israel.
> 6: Then he took the book of the covenant and read it in the hearing of the people; and they said, "All that the Lord has spoken we will do, and we will be obedient."

Note the people acknowledge that God was speaking to and through Moses. This "wrote down all the words of the Lord" action is thought to be the beginnings of what we have today as the first five books of the Bible called the Pentateuch.

Moses uses the "Love" Word

The "Love" word in describing God's relationship with man is mentioned the second time in the Bible in the Book of Deuteronomy. In this case Moses uses it in Deuteronomy to describe God's favor on the Israelites.

> Deut 4:37 Because He loved your forefathers and chose their descendants after them, He brought you out of Egypt by His Presence and his great strength, NIV
>
> Deut 7:8 But it was because the LORD loved you and kept the oath he swore to your forefathers that he brought you out with a mighty hand and redeemed you from the land of slavery, from the power of Pharaoh king of Egypt. NIV
>
> Deut 10:15 Yet the LORD set his affection on your forefathers and loved them, and he chose you, their descendants, above all the nations, as it is today. NIV

Thus, as I see it, God covenanted through love with man to provide a means of communication with Him, to provide reconciliation to Him and to provide a means of approaching Him available to each and every human.

All these features were embodied in the advent of Jesus Christ and fulfilled by Him as Christ became the sin-bearer for us all; provided we make the choice to accept this love offering from our creator God.

CHAPTER 7

The Grace Covenant

We see clear Prophetic evidence of the advent of Jesus in Jeremiah 31:31, declaring the coming of a new covenant

> Jer 31:31-33
> 31 "The time is coming," declares the LORD, "when <u>I will make a new covenant</u> with the house of Israel and with the house of Judah.
> 32 <u>It will not be like the covenant</u> I made with their forefathers when I took them by the hand to lead them out of Egypt, because they broke my covenant, though I was a husband to them," declares the LORD.
> 33 "<u>This is the covenant I will make</u> with the house of Israel after that time," declares the LORD. <u>"I will put my law in their minds and write it on their hearts.</u> I will be their God, and they will be my people. NIV

Thus it is my opinion that God, who spoke directly (held conversation – see Num 12:8) to Adam, Noah, Abram, qnd Moses (Aaron?) and carried out the Abram covenant until the birth of Jesus which I choose to call the "new heart" covenant, had finished with the preparation and was ready "in the fullness of time" to make His sacrifice. God was ready to visit the earth in the body like one of His created beings, exposed to the same carnal sin that all men and women face.

The New Heart Covenant

There is evidence in the Old Testament that of all God's concerns about our individual behavior He is most concerned about the content and intent of our "heart." To the wayward Children of Israel God had this to say about the "heart" and the "covenant."

> Deut 4:29-31
> 29 But if from there you seek the LORD your God, you will find him if you look for him with all your heart and with all your soul. 30 When you are in distress and all these things have happened to you, then in later days you will return to the LORD your God and obey him. 31 For the LORD your God is a merciful God; he will not abandon or destroy you or forget the covenant with your forefathers, which he confirmed to them by oath.
> NIV

God implores us to love Him with all our "heart."

Why?

Because He knows that our life can only be lived to the fullest while we are accumulating all the blessings He has for us, if we are in a close relationship with Him and that this relationship comes from the very depths of our heart.

Deut 6:4-6
4 Hear, O Israel: The LORD our God, the LORD is one.
5 Love the LORD your God with all your heart and with all your soul and with all your strength. 6 These commandments that I give you today are to be upon your hearts.

We could refer to God as "The Great Heart Examiner."

God is continually seeking "the pure of heart." I believe that as God continually examines our deeds He reaches decisions in real time regarding our relationship with Him thus He is totally focused on the inner man; He is focused on our "heart."

Let's ponder a few "heart" scriptures out of the 777 references to "heart" and "hearts" found in the NIV Bible.

The references in the "Positive:"

Prov 21:2 All a man's ways seem right to him, but the LORD weighs the heart. NIV

Jer 17:10 "I the LORD search the heart and examine the mind, to reward a man according to his conduct, according to what his deeds deserve." NIV

Jer 24:7 I will give them a heart to know me, that I am the LORD. They will be my people, and I will be their God, for they will return to me with all their heart. NIV

Ezek 36:26 I will give you a new heart and put a new spirit in you; I will remove from you your heart of stone and give you a heart of flesh. NIV

Matt 5:8 Blessed are the pure in heart, for they will see God. NIV

2 Chron 6:30 Forgive, and deal with each man according to all he does, since you know his heart (for you alone know the hearts of men), 31 so that they will fear you and walk in your ways all the time they live in the land you gave our fathers. NIV

2 Chron 16:9 For the eyes of the LORD range throughout the earth to strengthen those whose hearts are fully committed to him. NIV

1 Chron 29:17 I know, my God, that you test the heart and are pleased with integrity. NIV

Negative Style References:

Gen 6:5 The LORD saw how great man's wickedness on the earth had become, and that every inclination of the thoughts of his heart was only evil all the time. NIV

Deut 30:17 But if your heart turns away and you are not obedient, and if you are drawn away to bow down to other gods and worship them, 18 I declare to you this day that you will certainly be destroyed. NIV

1 Kings 11:4 As Solomon grew old, his wives turned his heart after other gods, and his heart was not fully

devoted to the LORD his God, as the heart of David his father had been. NIV

Isa 29:13 These people come near to me with their mouth and honor me with their lips, but their hearts are far from me. Their worship of me is made up only of rules taught by men. NIV

Job 36:13 "The godless in heart harbor resentment; even when he fetters them, they do not cry for help.
14 They die in their youth, NIV

Ps 14:1 The fool says in his heart, There is no God." NIV

Prov 11:20 The LORD detests men of perverse heart but he delights in those whose ways are blameless. NIV

Prov 16:5 The LORD detests all the proud of heart. Be sure of this: They will not go unpunished. NIV
Prov 17:20 A man of perverse heart does not prosper; he whose tongue is deceitful falls into trouble. NIV

Prov 26:24 A malicious man disguises himself with his lips,
but in his heart he harbors deceit. 25 Though his speech is charming, do not believe him, for seven abominations fill his heart. NIV

Matt 15:18 <u>But the things that come out of the mouth come from the heart</u>, and these make a man 'unclean.' 19 <u>For out of the heart come evil thoughts</u>, murder, adultery, sexual immorality, theft, false testimony, slander. NIV

Why all the "heart" scripture?

I offer it as introduction to a very important concept on prayer and the interventional power of prayer in altering the "suffering circumstances" sin has brought our way.

Premise one – we are sinners, one and all.

Premise two – God wishes it otherwise.

Premise three – God forgives sin. John 3:16

Premise four – if our "heart" is right with Him.

Before I pose a question on God's answers to prayer I would like to point out that while we may see our death as a believer as a dreaded thing God does not.

This is not to say that God does not see and feel through His love our sorrow at the death of a loved one or dear friend, but God knows that one of His believers is to be present with Him in a glorious place and thus He knows that those who die in Christ will be gloriously blessed and much better off in the Heaven prepared for them.

God's objective view of death for such a one is "it is reward time, come live with me."

God and Prayer

Now the big question; "Why is it, that God seemingly answers some prayers and not others?"

Why do we see Him answer favorably one prayer of one individual and seemingly not favorably answer the same prayer in what seems to us the same circumstance in another person's life?

In truth I do not know, but I offer the following logic as something to ponder.

In the first place I do not believe God busies himself trying to find ways to punish us for our everyday sin; such takes care of itself. I believe the consequences of sin were part of God's creating actions, thus are automatic and in place, rather I prefer to believe God is busy trying to figure out how He can turn our eyes to Him so we will leave our bent to sin behind. In the instance of a non-believer God is busy working to bring that non-believer into a relationship with Him through Jesus Christ. To so do He leaves no stone unturned. Does "no stone unturned" mean bad things can happen. The short answer is "Yes;" bad things are part and parcel of "the consequences" I am speaking of.

God sends messengers (people) into our lives to give us examples and leadership on how to come to Him. He is always there, in love with all, crying within as He waits for His created ones to come "wading out" of the consequences of rejecting Him and come home to Him one soul at a time.

The Holy Spirit is God's great "convector of sin" and is constantly at work on a believer's heart. Call it a guilty conscious or our inner desire to live sin free if you like but such is of God and directed by God if we are in truth a believer.

If an individual experiences no such "conscious tweaking" from God when knowingly committing sin, then the concern should be "am I really a follower of God or am I merely masquerading?"

As He does this "tweaking" I believe God is constantly looking at our heart; looking for that small change, that "glitter of guilt" we will carry as a result of our sin. Seeing this gives Him hope as He continuously attempts to persuade us to work to leave sin. As we sin I believe He is at work on our "conscious" attempting to place there a sense of remorse that will move us to repentance and the blessing of a closer walk with Him.

There is of course another consideration and that is "does the sinning believer have a Biblical understanding of what constitutes a sin against God?" I fear that too many believers are not very well schooled in what actions or inactions constitute sin.

The way a believer obtains these guidelines is through Bible study. A believer who engages in no

Bible study remains an infant in Christ thus not having a full knowledge of what constitutes "sin against God."

Per chance one is not a believer then the same Holy Spirit is present trying to urge that searching one to go ahead and accept Him. God is not willing that one should perish.

> 2 Peter 3:9
> 9 The Lord is not slack concerning his promise, as some men count slackness; but is longsuffering to us-ward, not willing that any should perish, but that all should come to repentance. KJV

It would take another book to define the spiritual aspects and the elements of sin but there are basically two types of sin; omission and commission. Sins of commission are basically those that break God's commandments on how we should live and interface with our fellow man and sins of omission are those things we should be doing in the name of God in service to our fellowman that we fail to do.

It is usually true we believers do a better job living up to the "thou shalt not" commandments of God than we do in being a servant to our fellowman. Much of the sinning that goes on in many Christian lives falls into the latter category. Often we merely fail to recognize an opportunity to serve. If recognized we fail to allocate time in our busy schedules to render to those in need of the assistance God would have us give them. In short, in the "lives a good life" category we do better than we do in the "serve others" category.

I believe that since God is always looking at the "heart;" and if finding there a "right minded and right hearted person in the flurries of sin" He patiently spends His time trying to extricate that individual from that sin through various kinds of positive influences. I base this stance on the scripture stated nature of God that He is "longsuffering" us-ward. If He fails to cause us to part with that sin, then the not so nice consequences of that sin ultimately will prevail and the individual will surely suffer as a result.

Since He loves us deeply as He does this work I believe where He sees remorse and repentance in the heart of a believer He intervenes in a manner that eases the consequences of that sin. Perhaps He eases the embarrassment of it all or He eases the consequences. But, I believe only if He sees and feels a proper amount of sincere heart contained grief and remorse over that sin along with sincere repentance and a prayer for forgiveness for that sin.

God's "prayer answering decisions" to some degree may well be products of what He finds in our heart through a God administered EKG of the heart. In modern vernacular God is continually conducting on each believer "a spiritual heart scan."

Stated again, if in that "scan" God finds a heart grieving to be right with Him, though in sin, that individual can through faith and prayer gain assistance from God in the here and now to remove themselves from the sin. Thus when God can see dread and remorse in the heart of a believer caught in the clutches of sin proffered by Satan I believe God works in answer to prayer to the sinner's advantage to ease consequences because of His love for us. I believe this because I do not believe God takes any pleasure in seeing His Satan entrapped truly repentant believer suffer. I had rather believe that God weeps along side His child who is sincerely attempting to extricate themselves from a besetting sin.

If on the other hand God sees a sinner with a calloused unreceptive heart then He leaves that individual to the continued consequences of that sin, waiting on the day when the full consequences of the sin weighs so heavily that there is a turning to God and that heart awakens. When God sees a "heart awakening" there is rejoicing in heaven.

God's answer to our prayers are, "yes" or "no" and these answers come in God's timing. While I believe the "heart condition" is a factor I also feel there are a number of other factors. I once read a book on prayer that suggested at least 11 reasons why God might not answer a specific prayer. God is God and I believe He has our best interest in His mind as he considers our petitions. Then He acts in His timing, not ours, if He considers our prayer in fact in earnest and persistent in nature.

CHAPTER 8

The polarities of - Health & Sickness

Living on our Created Earth

Ever since Adam and Eve were expelled from the Garden of Eden the human race has been living with the consequences. The nature of our lives, the human condition if you will, was preset by God in the creation.

The best we can do is to work to improve our living standard through the "subduing of the earth." This we have been working to accomplish since the days of Adam. It is obvious that all cultures if given education can make technological advances that improve on the human condition.

Through all this and the remarkable advances made in the medical professions, especially in the past 100 years, as humans we nonetheless must endure the polarities of health and sickness.

Health & Sickness

Another big "Why" Question – "If, as I say, God is so much for and into love, "why" would the all knowing and benevolent God I have described allow sickness and suffering in this world He created?"

Why do innocent babies suffer from sickness? What purpose could that possibly have?

Why does God allow innocent children to starve to death in countries where there is famine and destitution?

Why does God seemingly sit by and allow catastrophes to occur that maim and kill so many? Why not just create a place where there is no sickness, no famine, no starvation and let humanity live there?

Well guess what; that is exactly what He did when he created the Garden of Eden. Eden was that kind of place. Everything was furnished, food, water, nice weather; a place of absolute innocence.

And since God created man with His "unlimited love" He gave man a completely free will. I postulate this total latitude God gave His creation to choose good or evil, defines the immensity of God's love for man. In the creation He loved us so much that he gave us total freedom to do whatever we would like even to the far reaches of evil extremes. Though this appears as a downside to God's generosity in creation, it is in fact, only logical and is critical to the propagation of agape love.

Why is that?

I believe this is logical for the following reason. Since God created man to demonstrate His love and to solicit man's reciprocal love, the more freedom God allowed, the more meaningful to God would be man's love when returned to God. Thus it is our God given choice to love God or to deny God.

Be assured God could have created man where we would be something like Angels but He did not. But God sought to create man in such a way that when man makes the choice to love the creator God, such a choice will be based on a volunteered selfless, "God centered love" that by its very nature would be much more gratifying and pleasing to God. Having given that free latitude to "love God" to us, His giving and our accepting would be much more a blessing to God, than if man were created with emotional limits that somehow forced man to love God.

Or perhaps it would be better stated to say that were God to have created man with a fixed disposition to love God then the blessing to God when we return His love would be less inspiring to Him. Less inspiring than as it is now as he sees those of us who do love Him with a free will come to Him. Not because in creation He orchestrated it as a non-choice, but rather because we trust in Him and place our love on Him with our own uninhibited free will.

To illustrate this point Jesus told the parable of the lost sheep.

> Luke 15: Then Jesus told them this parable:
> 4 "Suppose one of you has a hundred sheep and loses one of them. Does he not leave the ninety-nine in the open country and go after the lost sheep until he finds it?
> 5 And when he finds it, he joyfully puts it on his shoulders
> 6 and goes home. Then he calls his friends and neighbors together and says, 'Rejoice with me; I have found my lost sheep.'
> 7 I tell you that in the same way there will be more rejoicing in heaven over one sinner who repents than over ninety-nine righteous persons who do not need to repent. NIV

Note the "...rejoicing in Heaven..." in verse 7 over just one person who repents and begins to love God. This very elegantly illustrates the point of why God created us with an absolute free will.

Joy in heaven surges when repentance takes place and one of His created beings turns to Him in love.

What does all this have to do with the subject of sickness and health? If we go back to Adam and think a moment an additional question is seen. Did God create Adam as a physically imperfect or physically perfect being?

I believe perfect. It is logical that God created Adam with no physical flaws; he was a perfect biological creation with no dispensation to physical disease of any kind.

We already know that the human body is a wonderfully made biological organism with powers of automatic food digestion, automatic nutrient extraction, automatic breathing, and automatic temperature control, and automatic chemical balance control, automatic reflexes to protect our bodies, automatic defense systems to ward off disease and automatic healing of minor and many major wounds.

This list pointing out the automatic nature of our body is but a partial list. There are many more automatic systems at work in our bodies at all times even while we sleep. In short we are a walking, talking, intelligent thinking, and biologically automatic operating organism. We are indeed a miracle of creation; even more than that; we have the power to pro-create. Being created male and female we have the ability to create more of ourselves with instructions from God to do so.

Sickness Enters

If, as I say, Adam was created perfectly then how did disease enter the scene? I believe in the following manner.

Disease entered the scene through man's conscious and unconscious failure to follow God's instructions. This failure came in at least five ways:

1. the disobedience of Adam and Eve and their relegation from the Garden of Eden to tilling the soil for food;
2. allowing our food intake to be contrary to God's instruction,
3. various forms of immorality as we too often turn from God following that "free will" that we allow to prevail into sin,
4. health consequences caused by the violation of God's instructions regarding sexual and other activities,
5. and finally through modern day man made chemicals that impinge on our DNA and cause various cellular mutations to form.

God's Diet for Man

For food, from Adam's day until after the days of Noah, God instructed man to use only the nuts, fruits and plants for food. See Genesis Gen 1:29-30.

> Gen 1:29 Then God said, "I give you every seed-bearing plant on the face of the whole earth and every tree that has fruit with seed in it. They will be yours for food.
> 30 And to all the beasts of the earth and all the birds of the air and all the creatures that move on the ground--everything that has the breath of life in it--I give every green plant for food." And it was so. NIV
> Gen 2:15 The LORD God took the man and put him in the Garden of Eden to work it and take care of it.

> 16 And the LORD God commanded the man, "You are free to eat from any tree in the garden;
> 17 but you must not eat from the tree of the knowledge of good and evil, for when you eat of it you will surely die." NIV

Given the above instructions what did man do? Let's take a look.

In Genesis 2:17 God instructed Adam not to eat of the tree of knowledge of good and evil, but man did not obey. What was to be the consequences if man disobeyed? "...you will surely die."

I wish to point out something here that many readers of the Bible fail to see. God instructed Adam in this. God did not instruct Eve. Eve wasn't even created until verse 22 of Chapter 1 and verse 21 of Chapter 2. Genesis Chapter 2 tells us that Adam was put in charge of caring for the Garden in verse 15 while it was not until verse 20 that Eve was created.
It is not recorded as to who instructed Eve regarding the forbidden fruit; perhaps it was Adam who was responsible to inform Eve. Or it could be Adam failed to adequately motivate Eve to obey in this and the Serpent used her lack of first hand knowledge and commitment as an entrapment.

In fact, we do not know, but we see in Chapter 3 how events unfolded.

> Gen 3:1 Now the serpent was more crafty than any of the wild animals the LORD God had made. He said to

> the woman, "Did God really say, 'You must not eat
> from any tree in the garden'?"
> 2 The woman said to the serpent, "We may eat fruit
> from the trees in the garden,
> 3 but God did say, 'You must not eat fruit from the tree
> that is in the middle of the garden, and you must not
> touch it, or you will die.'" NIV

> Gen 3:6 When the woman saw that the fruit of the tree was good for food and pleasing to the eye, and also desirable for gaining wisdom, she took some and ate it. She also gave some to her husband, who was with her, and he ate it.
> 7 Then the eyes of both of them were opened, NIV

Careful reading leaves the possibility that Adam did not realize just what Eve who had harvested the fruit was serving Adam for food.

In any case the absolute freedom of choice God gave His creation allowed Adam and Eve to rapidly disobey God. Both then suffered a traumatic emotional and physical setback. Their perfect bodies now had to deal with the life-altering effect of hardship.

I believe God created our bodies to function at peak efficiency (properly) only when we are in complete spiritual accord with the creator. You see, as implied above we are an automatic physiological, psychological, biological operational system. Unless we individually properly manage our heart, mind, soul and strength (remember those words?) we will never be all that God intended us to be; for it is in activating these four aspects of living that give us the power to be "fully engaged in living" as God intended.

A significant part of this accord with God has to do with diet and exercise. Improper diet has been shown to cause DNA mutations. And lack of exercise allows our bodies to atrophy ever so slightly day by day and over time significant physical limitations set in. We see in the Bible in the book of Genesis and Leviticus that God went to great pains to instruct man in the proper foods to eat.

<u>God Changes the Diet of Noah's Descendants</u>

At creation God specified man's food sources as follows in Genesis 1:29 and 30.

> Gen 1:29: Then God said, "Behold, I have given you every plant yielding seed that is on the surface of all the earth, and every tree which has fruit yielding seed; it shall be food for you.
> 30: and to every beast of the earth and to every bird of the sky and to every thing that moves on the earth <u>which has life</u>, I have given every green plant for food," and it was so.

So in the above man gets both, nuts, seeds and green plants. Though it may seem on reading that God gave the green plant only to the beasts and birds but note that He also allowed all "<u>which has life</u>" (includes man) to eat of green things. This also confirmed in Genesis 9:3 below.

After the flood God changed man's diet and gave man all things, plant and animal flesh for food without restrictions.

> Gen 9:1 Then God blessed Noah and his sons, saying to them, "Be fruitful and increase in number and fill the earth."
> 2 "The fear and dread of you will fall upon all the beasts of the earth and all the birds of the air, upon every creature that moves along the ground, and upon all the fish of the sea; they are given into your hands."
> 3 "Everything that lives and moves will be food for you. Just as I gave you the green plants, I now give you everything." NIV

Thus following these days men could eat all living things as food, yet later we see in Leviticus God amended these instructions limiting once again man's food intake with some detailed specifics. In the first 10 Chapters of Leviticus God gives instruction regarding sin offerings.

In this discourse to Moses God commanded something specific that in the light of today's medical science on the ravages of high cholesterol could seem to have been purposely used by God to protect the health of His people.

In all fairness to other views, many people believe that these Biblical laws do not apply in modern times, arguing that the lack of refrigeration in ancient times dictated much of the Biblical requirements. This supposition is likely true to some degree but in fact we have no hard information either way. Thus you see my position is slanted toward modern day application of scientific knowledge being valid as I apply that knowledge to the Leviticus laws of diet.

In the eleventh chapter of Leviticus God gives instructions on limiting the eating of animals in 46 verses. These instructions are very specific and detailed. Significant among these instructions in Leviticus you will notice is God's "animal fat" instructions.

The Fat is the Lord's.

> Lev 3:17 "'This is a lasting ordinance for the generations to come, wherever you live: You must not eat any fat or any blood.'" NIV

Again in the 7th Chapter of Leviticus we see:

> Lev 7:22 The LORD said to Moses,
> 23 "Say to the Israelites: 'Do not eat any of the fat of cattle, sheep or goats.
> 24 The fat of an animal found dead or torn by wild animals may be used for any other purpose, but you must not eat it.
> 25 Anyone who eats the fat of an animal from which an offering by fire may be made to the LORD must be cut off from his people.
> 26 And wherever you live, you must not eat the blood of any bird or animal.
> 27 If anyone eats blood, that person must be cut off from his people.'" NIV

Note: In the above verse God said "for the generations to come" and did not say "until refrigeration is invented."

As one reads Leviticus there are abundant references to animal fat being burned on the Alter for sin sacrifice. It was not to be eaten, it was to be offered to God, yet today, humans consume the fat of these animals at alarming rates and we find generally from medical research that animal fat is not a healthy food to consume.

I should note though that modern nutritionists tell us that some fat in the diet is essential to good health. Note, in spite of this requirement, I would suggest that animal fat is not needed to fill this role. There are a number of other fats from nuts and seeds available; coconut and olive oil being common ones.

God, also in Leviticus restricted some animals from the diet of man for the first time.

> Lev 11:1 The LORD said to Moses and Aaron,
> 2 "Say to the Israelites: 'Of all the animals that live on land, these are the ones you may eat... NIV

From your Bible read the 11th Chapter of Leviticus to find all the food instructions given to the Israelites.

DNA Altered?

Do I think that sinful man obeyed to the letter God's instructions on eating after receiving them?

No I do not.

Some men not having the permitted foods available likely ate what was available and suffered the consequences.

Was DNA altered? Perhaps; science is still working on this question but my thought is that in due time science will find DNA altered.

Life circumstances that affect our DNA are being discovered daily; for instance it is now known that ultraviolet light, tobacco and certain common chemicals can cause DNA mutations. Thus our DNA can be altered by exposure to these and assuredly others as yet unknown environmental hazards.

A personal example is that during my engineering career I was exposed to five things that later proved to be carcinogens; Asbestos, Carbon Tetrachloride, Benzene, Toluene and Phenol. At the time I was exposed nothing was known of these chemicals to alarm us to the potential dangers to health.

As a result I am confident that one day in the future science will discover other chemicals commonly used today that will be banned because of the threat to DNA mutations and other side effects. The Federal Food and Drug Administration (FDA) attempts to protect us from dangerous prescription drugs; but even so occasionally we hear of the FDA withdrawing a drug from the market that has proven to be too dangerous to human health. One can see chemical exposures occurring everyday with the household chemicals, and hair sprays we use, and foods we ingest containing chemicals such as food preservatives and one that has gotten a lot of publicity; animal growth hormones.

However, as you will see from the information provided below, even our DNA has a God created mechanism that repairs "most" DNA mutations. This is another example of how we are automatically controlled by the marvelous and miracle laden anatomy we have been given.

Note in the previous paragraph the word "most." Some mutants make it through to become threats to our general health. The following information on DNA was gathered from the internet.
Quotes:

> *DNA contains the instructions needed for a living organism to grow and function. It tells cells exactly what role they should play in the body.*
> *It holds instructions to make your heart cells beat, your limbs form in the correct place, for the immune system fight infection, and for our digestive system digest our food.*
>
> *DNA carries instructions In (Science assigned) codes using four alpha designations;: G, A, T and C. The sequence of these letters used properly is known as the genetic code. A molecule of DNA resembles a twisted ladder. Each rung of the ladder is made up of two DNA letters. A always binds to T and G always binds to C. The binding of the letters causes the whole*

molecule to coil up into a spiral staircase-like structure called a double helix. Source - ***http://www.members.optusnet.com.au/~acceptance/YourPurposeWeb/DNAEncoding.htm***

I sought an answer to "can extreme emotional distress cause mutations in DNA. I found the following information on the internet which is one person's opinion.

The only way that DNA can be permanently "changed" is through mutation. Agents such as smoking can definitely cause mutational changes. This is the basis for smoking causing cancer. While drugs, alcohol, & intense emotional states can all be detrimental to the body, these effects are not generally mediated by a change in DNA sequence, i.e. mutations. However, I think that some drugs, particularly those whose production & distribution are not regulated, including alcohol, could potentially cause DNA damage, especially if abused/over- used. But there are many other environmental agents, such as certain solvents, UV rays in sunlight, radiation sources, & chemical contaminants of drinking water that can cause DNA changes/mutations, too. In short, DNA can definitely be changed by outside stimuli...., but not likely by long-term emotions. Source - **http://www.madsci.org/posts/archives/may2000/957310344.Ge.r.html**

Note the underlines words, "...but not likely..."; in other words we do not know!

The following article appeared on the internet web site of British Broadcasting Corporation News on November 17, 2005.

Genes can be 'changed' by foods

What we eat may influence our health by changing specific genes, researchers believe.

Several studies in rodents have shown that nutrients and supplements can change the genetics of animals by switching on or off certain genes.

It is not clear whether foods do the same in humans, but an article in New Scientist says there is good reason to believe they do.

In the future, diseases might be reversed by diet in this way, it says.

Modifying DNA

While many disorders in humans are caused by mutations to DNA, a few, including some cancers, occur when genes are switched on or off.

There are thousands of genes in the body, but not all of them are active.

Scientists have been looking at what factors might control gene activity and have found some evidence to suggest that diet is important.

In a recent animal experiment, adult rats were made to behave differently by injecting them with a specific amino acid called L-methionine.

After the injections, the animals were less confident when exploring new environments and produced higher levels of stress hormones.

The change to their behaviour occurred because the amino acid altered the way the rat's genes were expressed.

L-methionine altered a gene for glucocorticoid that helps control the animal's response to stress, Moshe Szyf and his team from McGill University in Montreal, Canada, told a meeting on environmental epigenomics in November in Durham, North Carolina.

It added chemical tags, known as methyl groups, to the gene by a process called methylation.

The researchers are now looking to see if they can cause a positive rather than a negative behavioural change in animals using a naturally-occurring chemical called trichostatin A (TSA).

TSA causes the opposite effect to L-methionine on genes, stripping them of methyl groups.

Dr Szyf said his work showed how important subtle nutrients and supplements can be.

Animal research has also shown that a mother's diet can affect the level of DNA methylation and hence gene expression in offspring.

Professor Ian Johnson at the Institute of Food Research is investigating whether colon cancer in humans might be triggered by diet through DNA methylation. His team is studying healthy people before this cancer starts.

He said: "It's quite a strong possibility that nutrients might cause DNA changes. We think diet may have a role to play as a regulator in genes.

"Ultimately one would want to chose diets that would give you the most beneficial pattern of DNA methylation in the gut. But it is too early to say that we know the dietary strategy to do that.

"We need much more research.

"Genes regulate all the processes in the body and things that change gene expression, therefore, may be linked to a number of health issues other than cancer too."

He said one nutrient that scientists believe might influence methylation is folate or folic acid. A deficiency in folate levels has been linked to an increased risk of developing some adult cancers, including breast and colon.

We have many people alive today that testify to the benefits of a changed diet on their general health. One of note is Jordan S. Rubin who at age 19 and 20 was reduced to a wheel chair with 19 diagnosed diseases.

But in a step of faith and in Bible study about the diet God gave to man in the book of Leviticus and other places, Jordan took action. With the aid of his parents he changed his diet, and conquered the diseases that had beset him. He has written a book about these experiences titled, "The Makers Diet" that is getting a lot of publicity as I write these lines.

CHAPTER 9

The polarities of: Sin – Sinless

There is a "behavioral sin" spectrum (active polarity) we live within on this earth. All live along it, saved or unsaved. At one end is the behavior of the Perfect Son of God representing the LOVE of God through Jesus Christ. At the other end is Satan, representing perfection in evil behavior.

-S p e c t r u m-

Satan<-------------------<<^ - ME - ^>>------------------> Jesus
Total Evil Perfect Love

The issue is always about whose neighborhood are we living in? This "Jesus on the right, Satan on the left" concept illustrates the choices we must make in our mental and physical behavior.

Both Jesus and Satan, stand on the opposite ends of this spectrum with welcoming arms out-stretched, beckoning us to come; to Jesus to give us salvation and everlasting eternal love; or to Satan to give us carnal fulfillment and spiritual death. Which will it be? All must decide! Putting it off is a decision as well. Even after having accepted God's plan of redemption, believers being of a sinful nature along with non-believers live at some point along the width of this spectrum, and as we live minute by minute we in fact move, to and fro, never static for as long as our mind takes us into the many Satan set traps for sinful thought if not deed. The believer's job is one of sin recognition and self removal, with acceptance of God's plan for repentance and prayer for forgiveness.

Life Decisions

Life, as God created it, has three great decisions to be made.

These are: 1. will you know God through Jesus; 2. whom will be your life's mate; and 3. what will be your life's work?

Let's take them in "3 - 2 – 1" order.

3. What will be your life's work?

Obviously this answer depends on the answer you give to question 1.

If we choose not to believe, we have a full range of choices on profession. Those who choose an occupation on Satan's side of commerce may, later in life be faced with a career change and I have seen a number of these changes made after one accepts Christ.

It is common and correct to make such career changing decisions. If you are declaring yourself on God's side of life then one must also declare on God's side of commerce.

a. Interventional Prayer

Interestingly, many who by default (putting off the decision for Christ), may not be aware of a force at work in their lives that may at any time cause a change in your earlier decision for inaction. That is the power of prayer of those who love them and who are believers who are praying for their deliverance into the joy of knowing Christ. Sadly our loved ones may pray for us for years only to see us fail to ever make a decision for Christ. But, happily many tell emotionally moving stories of life changing experiences when they decided to claim Christ as Savior that came as a result of prayer by loved ones.

In such cases as these, whether or not one ends up accepting Christ, I believe is a matter of the heart. If in our "heart" we have sought to play games with God then he can and does withdraw His call on our spirit and following this event one cannot become a believer. For at some point God has allowed Satan to remove even the desire. Sadly I share that I have seen many cases of inability to believe that could have been so caused by Satan. A few even desperately wanted to accept Christ and actually told me so but said they simply could not for reasons even they did not understand.

These may well have stepped over God's boundaries of His extended longsuffering and He gives them over to indecision at best and debauchery at worst. One such scripture on this subject is found in Romans 1:18-32.

When acceptance of Christ comes to an individual it is often is found "on the heal" of some type of life altering trauma that occurs. The trauma then causes a time of re-examination of life's priorities and precipitating from that follows the long delayed decision to repent and follow Christ.

The trauma or adversity, of course, is an event or events that are nothing more than God's laws at work as they inevitably address the consequences of sin in our life and that of our ancestors or in some cases it can be the mere exposure we or our parents or even perhaps grandparents have had to unknown chemical assailants.

b. The Believer's Occupation

Our occupation is just one area of service to God.

Personally I view my occupation that God has made possible for me to pursue as my "God given ministry." I do it to His glory always looking for another chance to serve and to bring a witness of Christ to any others that I may encounter. Such situations are of God and He can use us to point someone else to Him. For God to be successful in this enterprise we must be aware of this potential and alert to actively look for opportunities that God sends our way.

Sin at Will?

Some have asked, "As long then, as we faithfully serve others can we then sin at will?" Go back to James 1:27 and read the last few words. "...and keep himself unspotted from the world." That would be keeping free of "sin spots."

2. Who will be your life's mate?

This decision will seem to some easy. Just wait until he/she comes along and if we fall in love, that's it.

The scripture talks of "believers being equally yoked" in marriage.

> 2 Cor 6:14-17
> 14 Do not be yoked together with unbelievers. For what do righteousness and wickedness have in common? Or what fellowship can light have with darkness?

> 15 What harmony is there between Christ and Belial? What does a believer have in common with an unbeliever?
> 16 What agreement is there between the temple of God and idols? For we are the temple of the living God. As God has said: "I will live with them and walk among them, and I will be their God, and they will be my people."
> 17 "Therefore come out from them and be separate, says the Lord. NIV

Just what does this scripture mean?

Right off one might venture that it means that both husband and wife believe in God and have accepted Jesus Christ as Lord and Savior. Such a position is the only proper starting place for being equally yoked in a Christian marriage. For these spiritual platforms will be the foundation on which you will build your "life long" relationship.

However, there are a few other important moral and family based values that you will do well to be aligned on prior to marriage. One can make a list and please allow me to make an incomplete one.

1. The first is "are we going to have children and if so how many?"
2. Are we both going to have jobs and work outside the home?
3. If so and we are planning children; there is a conflict of interests between jobs and children for parental time; so how are we going to

solve that area of potential differences in priorities?

4. What about money? Who is going to pay the bills? Are we going to have a savings account? Are all accounts going to be in common?
5. Are we going to tithe our income? If so on what basis? Ten percent of what sum?
6. What are we going to live in? Are we going to rent or buy?
7. Are we going to be regular in Worship attendance? If so what denomination will we be members of? Are we going to be active in a Bible Study class with other couples? Are we going to take positions of responsibility if asked?
8. What about our transportation? Are we going to have two automobiles? If so what type, model and year?
9. Is ether of us going to continue our education? What are the potential problems this might create?
10 . What about credit? How much monetary credit, if any, are we going to carry at any one time?
11 . In our spiritual walk are we going to serve others; if so in what ways? What charities are we going to support?
12. What about friends? Are we going to actively cultivate friendships of like minded people with whom we can fellowship and share life's journey?

13. What about family? Are we going to interface with both our families in an equal fashion?
14. What about hobbies? How about travel? How are we going to balance our spending among these?
15. What about children's sports and activities? How are we going to balance our participation as parents?

The above is not a complete list of all potential areas to be concerned with in working out our being "equally yoked" with our mate.

One could ask; "Are you sure anyone would ever get married if before hand they had to work out all these details?"

Perhaps not and that's OK also. However, such a possibility of not marrying does not remove the wisdom of discussing all these in some detail ahead of time so that there are fewer surprises after the wedding day and consequently more opportunity for unwanted conflict to be reduced.

I am not necessarily talking nuptial agreement here, but there could be cases where even this would be wise to create. The point is to maximize your opportunity for the marriage to work into the distant future.

A marriage is, if anything, a trust agreement. And trust can flourish more in an atmosphere of mutual understanding; one where each spouse has expectations of the other that are real and not supposed. How do we do all this? Talk, talk, talk on an agenda is my answer.

Now last and most important –

1. Will you know God through Jesus Christ?

This is the "Where do you plan to spend eternity Question?"

This decision is foundational to life and living a fulfilled life.

Many people start making life's big decisions without a spiritual foundation. This is like getting the cart before the horse; and life's issues and happenings end up causing us to be befuddled and confused, emotionally upside down and sometimes in emotional shambles.

All this because we went off on our journey in the wrong direction, subsequently finding ourselves wanting to change our course and finding it is not that easy. Our "God connection" (next chapter) foundation is missing and we simply founder in the morass of life's "unresolved leftover issues."

Actually question "One" is never waiting for an answer. We answer "no" by merely waiting or postponing the decision. Which is exactly what

Satan's alternate strategy is; "tell'em it is all true, just that now is not the time." This is the secondary strategy Satan uses for all those who are uncertain; not able to decide right now.

Satan's primary strategy is simply, "tell'em none of it is true; it is all false." Satan is very adept at using the Christian failures to ward off potential believers. Many there are who have been so diverted.

Our choice on Question One has everything to do with the nature and quality of our "fulfillment" in life. "Fulfillment has two aspects to it that are related to the reason for our being." One, "fulfillment" as offered by Satan is totally self centered; all about me and my worldly pleasures of material and carnal things.

"Fulfillment" as offered by God is all about others, a life of service to God via family, charitable giving, friends, serving the needy, with self taking last place.

A full portion of "life's pleasures" are built into God's plan in an even more powerful way than "sinful pleasures" are a part in Satan's plan.

Unless we have experienced the pleasure of helping others we cannot know what we are missing in finding fulfillment in God's purpose for your life. For instance from those who have had the experience to know of these things; sex in a loving and giving marriage is light-years ahead of sex outside of marriage as far as sexual fulfillment is concerned. Sex is God's grand design of pleasure to promote procreation for man and woman. This pleasure insures man does in fact "populate the earth." Misused it is disease laden and trite. Properly engaged in marital union, it becomes the highest of fulfillment. But even God's sanctioned marital sex does not bring God's total fulfillment. His total fulfillment comes in serving Him. Your mate is just one of those opportunities of serving.

When we accept Christ then our choice of our life's work has some moral limitations attached. As a believer one will not want to choose a profession that in any way promotes the work of Satan.

The challenge is to at last get it right and that can only happen after we acknowledge Jesus as our Master and Jesus as our Savior. Then just as God intended it, all things fall into place and the question posed on page 1 of "why?" comes into full focus.

It is then we can have hope of getting our human bent to sin under control.

CHAPTER 10

Satan's Role

There is no human derived evil thing, act, thought or grievous inaction that exceeds Satan in his pure ability to be evil and to cause evil things to happen. Try if you will to imagine the most evil circumstance that your human mind can conceive; once you have done that be assured that Satan is multiple times more evil than your thoughts.

Remember I am proposing evil was created to allow God's great love to be fully demonstrated, and to maximize His reward to those who love God. Therefore, if this is so, we must conclude that there is nothing of this world capable of being more evil than Satan. In order for Adam to choose to disobey God, Adam had to embrace the advice of Satan. Adam being created by God as intellectually perfect, we cannot but conclude that Satan must therefore possess tremendous powers of persuasion and allure. As punishment for this direct act of disobedience, and defiance of His creator's command, God expelled Adam and Eve from the Garden of Eden, the perfect place, to a life of toil, tilling the ground for food.

The Bible gives us the characteristics of Satan. He is a murderer and a liar.

Jesus speaking to unbelieving Jews said this in John 8:43-45:

> 43. Because you are unable to hear what I say. 44 You belong to your father, the devil, and you want to carry out your father's desire. He was a murderer from the beginning, not holding to the truth, for there is no truth in him. When he lies, he speaks his native language, for he is a liar and the father of lies. NIV

Satan is the tempter.

> Mark 1:12-13
> 12 At once the Spirit sent him out into the desert, 13 and he was in the desert forty days, being tempted by Satan. He was with the wild animals, and angels attended him.
> NIV

Satan seeks to afflict us.

> Luke 22:31-32
> 31 "Simon, Simon, Satan has asked to sift you as wheat.
> 32 But I have prayed for you, Simon, that your faith may not fail. And when you have turned back, strengthen your brothers." NIV

Evil masquerades as an apostle of Christ.

> 2 Cor 11:13-15
> 13 For such men are false apostles, deceitful workmen, masquerading as apostles of Christ. 14 And no

wonder, for Satan himself masquerades as an angel of light. 15 It is not surprising, then, if his servants masquerade as servants of righteousness. Their end will be what their actions deserve. NIV

Satan seeks to do us harm.

Rev 2:10

10 "Do not fear what you are about to suffer. Behold, the devil is about to cast some of you into prison, so that you will be tested, and you will have tribulation for ten days. Be faithful until death, and I will give you the crown of life. NASU

Satan is the great deceiver and accuser.

Rev 12:9-10

9 And the great dragon was thrown down, the serpent of old who is called the devil and Satan, who deceives the whole world; he was thrown down to the earth, and his angels were thrown down with him.

10 Then I heard a loud voice in heaven, saying, "Now the salvation, and the power, and the kingdom of our God and the authority of His Christ have come, for the accuser of our brethren has been thrown down, he who accuses them before our God day and night. NASU

Satan seeks to bring suffering to us.

1 Peter 5:8-10

8 Be of sober spirit, be on the alert. Your adversary, the devil, prowls around like a roaring lion, seeking someone to devour.

9 But resist him, firm in your faith, knowing that the same experiences of suffering are being accomplished by your brethren who are in the world.

BUT God gives us the promise of restoration.

> 10 After you have suffered for a little while, the God of all grace, who called you to His eternal glory in Christ, will Himself perfect, confirm, strengthen and establish you. NASU

In brief, I firmly believe it is Satan that brings all the evil things into this world including sickness; therefore when you see children suffering in starvation, seek answers to why in the role of Satan; in what areas has he successfully deceived to cause such affliction and illness?

Remember God asks us to be His. If we choose to live away from God following some form of idol (any pursuit other than to follow after God,) there are natural consequences and these are never pleasant! Furthermore, these consequences are foretold in the Bible.

Remember the second of the 10 commandments?

> Deut 5:8-10
> 8 "You shall not make for yourself an idol in the form of anything in heaven above or on the earth beneath or in the waters below.
> 9 You shall not bow down to them or worship them; for I, the LORD your God, am a jealous God, punishing the children for the sin of the fathers to the third and fourth generation of those who hate me,
> 10 but showing love to a thousand generations of those who love me and keep my commandments.
> NIV

This punishing spoken of in verse 9, I believe comes through the created but now naturally occurring consequences of not following God I have mentioned earlier. We must live with the aftermath of sin by our forebears as well as the consequences of our own sin.

The second commandment forbidding he making of idols is profound in promises of burdens to bear. We see the consequences of the violation of this commandment played out in the world every day as evil guides those seeking to remove freedom from the world stage.

As a consequence of Satan's work, there are starving children in Africa and other places, not because God is actively punishing these babies; rather this suffering is a direct consequence of the sins of the cultural forebears of the these children.

What then are we to do? The answer is clear; as believers we are to help relieve this suffering through evangelism, personal intervention and through giving of aid, both personal and governmental.

And notice the wonderful promise of verse 10. "...but showing love to a thousand generations of those who love me and keep my commandments." A thousand generations is something like 20 to 40 thousand years; a very long time on the scale of man's lifespan.

CHAPTER 11

The Nature of God

As believers we give our thoughts to God and worship Him and give Him credit for our blessings rightly so, but do we really know God's true characteristics? If not, how can we find out?

To better understand the God's "Grace" Covenant discussed in Chapter 8 it will be beneficial to do an assessment of the "characteristic nature of God." This is easily done because the Bible has multitudes of references to God's characteristics.

Allow me to share a scripture search on <u>*what God is like.*</u>

God is merciful, gracious, longsuffering, with goodness and mercy.

> *Ex 34:6 The LORD, the LORD God, merciful and gracious, longsuffering, and abounding in goodness and truth,*
> *7 keeping mercy for thousands, <u>forgiving iniquity and transgression and sin</u>, by no means clearing the guilty,*

> *visiting the iniquity of the fathers upon the children and the children's children to the third and the fourth generation."* NKJV

The words "...by no means clearing the guilty..." to me means if we choose to ignore God's sin offering thru Jesus, then it is by our own choice we have decided to reject God. We are then guilty of rejection and God will not, indeed cannot force us to love Him; God will NEVER reject me or you but it is always once and for all times our personal choice. But, again, when we do reject Him by way of His creation He chose to be powerless in forcing us to love Him in order to give that same love option the maximum meaning to Him and to us. But I also believe when He finds He is unable to clear the guilty it is with great anguish on His part

God wants our love. He commands it for our own good.

> Deut 6:5-6 Love the LORD your God with all your heart and with all your soul and with all your strength. NIV

God advises us to fear Him.

> Deut 6:13-15 Fear the LORD your God, serve him only and take your oaths in his name. 14 Do not follow other gods, the gods of the peoples around you;... NIV

God is jealous.

> Deut 6:15 for the LORD your God, who is among you, is a jealous God and his anger will burn against you,... NIV

God is merciful.

Deut 4:31 For the LORD your God is a merciful God; he will not abandon or destroy you or forget the covenant with your forefathers, which he confirmed to them by oath. NIV

God is faithful.

Deut 7:9-10
God is God; he is the faithful God, keeping his covenant of love to a thousand generations of those who love him and keep his commands. NIV

God constrains temptation.

1 Cor 10:13 And God is faithful; he will not let you be tempted beyond what you can bear. NIV

God is gracious and compassionate.

2 Chron 30:9 the LORD your God is gracious and compassionate. NIV

God is our refuge and strength and help.

Ps 46:1God is our refuge and strength, an ever-present help in trouble. NIV

God is holy.

Ps 99:9 the LORD our God is holy. NIV

God protects.

Ps 116 The LORD protects the simple-hearted; when I was in great need, he saved me. NIV

God is my salvation.

Isa 12:2 Surely God is my salvation; NIV

God is merciful and forgiving.

> Dan 9:9 The Lord our God is merciful and forgiving, NIV

God is just.

> 2 Thess 1:6 God is just: NIV

God is light.

> 1 John 1:5 God is light; in him there is no darkness at all. NIV

And finally God is love.

> 1 John 4:16 God is love. NIV

Two things about God's character are very clear under the Covenant of Moses.

One; under the old covenant in the Old Testament we see that God did-not, could not tolerate idolatry or evil men. Time and time again in the Books of Moses we see God decree all such people killed often including women and children; and to that end we see God empower the Israelites to successfully overpower the various evil and idol worshipping tribes Israel encountered. As far as the Israelites were concerned the power was theirs with a big "IF;" "IF" the Israelites were obedient to God and followed His wishes they would always prevail over their enemies. However, when they wandered from following Him to following idols He allowed them to be overcome by evil tribes and even taken into captivity.

Two; as hard as God was on the Canaanites and other idolatrous peoples He was often, at Moses' behest, quick to forgive the many transgressions against God by His chosen people the Israelites as they traveled in the wilderness those 40 years.

There are many warnings in the Books of Moses to the Israelites against forsaking their God. But sadly the Israelites receded into sin time after time after time ad-nauseam.

Personally I find it hard to have forgiving attitude toward them for they were repeatedly so callused but guess what; just as God forgave them He forgives any and all of us through earnest repentance! God despises a haughty attitude of self proclaimed strength and righteousness and warns of such. One such warning to the Israelites is found in -

> Deut 9:4 "Do not say in your heart when the Lord has driven them out before you, 'Because of my righteousness the Lord has brought me in to possess this land,' but it is because of the wickedness of these nations that the Lord is dispossessing them before you." NASV

CHAPTER 12

The God Connection

As human beings all wonder "what is our connection to the cosmos?" Are we to be burdened from birth to death with this ingrained wonderment about our origins to which there seems no answer? Are we merely pawns in a greater scheme? Is the future of this planet fixed in a meaningless time space dimension and it matters not our measly contribution as to the outcome on our planet? If by force of will in living our lives we put good above evil as individuals; will such make any difference in our final day?

OR-

Is everyone born with a God connection? Is there a grand plan and purpose for our individual lives? Did a higher being known to the cultures of the world as God, create what we know and have today for His benefit? If He did, what might that benefit be? Do we have any clues we can pick up on as we ponder these questions that will provide answers? Are there physical laws at work that we need to be tuned into?

If we need to be tuned in, what might the purpose be for the tuning?

Some ask, some live, some act, some react, some laze, some work, some smile, some frown, some stand, some sit, some run, some walk, some live, some die; in the meantime the "why" of it all remains. If there is an answer where can it be found?

I propose the "why" answer is found and the answer to life's purpose is "Love!" Agape love! With "Love" proposed as the answer, how can one test this hypothesis?

I believe we can test it through examination using the human trait of having the ability to impose logic; i.e., being logical. Of all things natural, it is only and solely the natural occurrence of the emotion "love" that comes even close to explaining the questions of "why are we here" posed above.

At once, "love" is both intensely personal and, for complete fulfillment to occur, love must also be selflessly "corporate" or "bi-lateral."

"Love in a single inward directional mode" ends up being selfish, frustrating and lifeless and ultimately filled with despair. But "love" felt and returned has at its very roots the highest form of human "fulfillment."

If then, "love" is so monumental in importance in the make up of all things; might "love" then be the purpose of our very existence?

The Christian Bible argues so.

Logic argues so.

A picture of a loving God, comes to me in the following as stated in fourth line of the Lord's Prayer given to us by His Son Jesus, "Thy will be done in Heaven as it is on earth."

Jesus clearly states "God's will is done in Heaven" and instructs us to ask in prayer for earth to become a heaven like place. In Heaven there is no sorrow, death, violence, sadness, sickness, nor any evil. In giving us the Lord's Prayer Jesus said to ask for it!

We are to pray for "Heaven on Earth."

Now tell me this, if Jesus in giving us the Lord's Prayer invoked Heaven on Earth, why should we believe any of this death, sickness, violence, sadness, sickness, and evil is or can be resulting from the "present or ongoing acts" of a loving but somehow vengeful God?

If true, did God nonetheless author the creation that surely includes all the above listed sorrows?

Answer - He did.

As argued earlier, logically, for God to create the possibility for pure love to exist, God also had to allow the opposite. And along with the evil opposite He also had to allow the not so nice consequences of that evil.

Even as God did this in the creation process He implores us to avoid Satan, and urges us to follow His teachings. God fully knows the consequences of evil and He does not want us to have to endure them. I submit that is God's created love in action.

I also submit we need to think of God in a manner that recognizes the pre-existence of sin's consequences; so to live is to be exposed to all that is and there are consequences for violating God's laws of Godly living.

And sometimes we even encounter the consequences of sin as innocent bystanders as someone else who violates God's laws of creation does something evil and the consequences of this evil act negatively effects our well being innocent though we be.

If we defy gravity for the sake of such defiance and take a fall from very high we will very likely die. Thusly dieing cannot and should not ever be construed as God's will for us. He wants us to be smart, not stupid to take such a jump thinking we can fly.

Yet we do similar acts all the time. We say; "That is fun, the flying part; it's the stopping part that hurts." When someone dies in such a manner one should never say it is/was the will of God that such a person die. In such cases it was our will not His that was fulfilled. God does allow our will to prevail even to our death. We recognize in similar cases but different circumstances death results from the violation of God's immutable laws. Considering the jumper illustration the human body is not built to sustain such a sudden stop at such a high velocity.

Likewise the human spirit is not designed to be fulfilled by acts of disobedience; rather by the acts of following God's moral urging. So come to Him, live for Him and enjoy the rewards of being in tune with God's will for your life where His blessings make life so much more fulfilling and enjoyable.

That is the way God created man and women; thus for the "love" of God to be brought to fruition where we accept His terms and the rewards flowing there from, there must also be as an opposite result of our denying Him and being exposed to the bad consequences.

These sin consequences are not something He waits on His throne to administer, but rather He sadly observes them happening following an act of denying His commandments or rules for living. The result or consequences of sin are in constant motion, they are irrefutable and irrevocable. They were here from the beginning. They are.

Does this mean all is pre-destined to be, negating of the need to engage in and enjoy the power of prayer in our everyday lives?

How Does Prayer Fit In?

The above argument sounds like all that happens can be viewed as our "fate" predicated on our living.

How could this be so and there still be power in prayer?

To answer this question we must do an analysis of prayer. Prayer offered to God can be for a number of reasons and offered in a number of conditions or situations. Once we make the decision for salvation through the sacrifices of Jesus and have become Children of God, we then can begin one of our ministries; the ministry of prayer.

Basic and first in priority is the prayer for salvation. This is a prayer of repentance and contrition. It is our saving prayer. During this prayer God's Holy Spirit that has been "knocking on our hearts door" can now walk in the door opened as one begins the prayer of salvation.

Second, in order to stay in relationship with God we must pray for forgiveness when we sin. Most of us know when we commit acts of overt sin, but Satan has an even more insidious type of sin He tempts us with. I will call it the "centered on self" sin that omits Christian service to and for others.

This sin is not so apparent to far too many Christian people. We may be faithful in Bible Study, faithful to live overt sin free for the most part and then leave a loving concern for opportunity to serve others completely out of our lives. In other words we fail to do those things God placed in our path "that we should walk in them." Ephesians 2:10b.

Third, is the prayer we utter for a consciousness of the opportunities for us to serve God that come our way day to day. This prayer is to follow the prayer of forgiveness of sin, overt and unknown. If we do this it is amazing what God will reveal to us as small opportunities during our day to day activities to serve Him. Part of this prayer of course is to be a faithful witness for Him. For sometimes in the most unlikely circumstances there will appear an opportunity to witness to an unsaved person. See 1st Peter 3:15

> 1st Peter 3:15. But sanctify Christ as Lord in your hearts, always being ready to make a defense to everyone who asks you to give an account for the hope that is in you, yet with gentleness and reverence.

Important, I feel in the above verse are two concepts – "be ready when asked," and to "do so with gentleness." This means to emphasize the love of God and not condemn those asking by your words, but utter words of love and encouragement gently explaining the plan of salvation. Always emphasizing the amazing love of God, and that God's greatest desire is that no person perish but all come to a saving knowledge of Him.

Fourth, is the prayer for God to intervene in situations or circumstances. Significant in the category of prayer is the prayer for physical healing. These situations can cover a wide variety of subjects and needs, with some even for release from the ordained consequences of some grievous sin.

Fifth, is prayer "for those" who may be persecuting us. Many times a Christian is persecuted and it is never known by the one persecuted. Such may be a suspicion but not known as a fact. At other times it is clear that persecution is a fact.

Jesus testified to the power of prayer and told us to pray; even teaching us a model prayer, which tells me we will do well to believe Him. Let's look at Jesus own comments on prayer and the importance of believing an answer will come. I will list these prayer scriptures in Biblical order as they appear in the Four Gospels beginning with The Gospel of Matthew.

<u>References to "Pray" in Matthew</u>

> Matt. 5:43: You have heard that it was said; You shall love your neighbor and hate your enemy. 44: But I say

to you, love your enemies and pray for those who persecute you.

Matt. 6:5 And when you pray, you are not to be as
hypocrites; for they love to stand and pray in the
synagogues and on the street corners, in order to be
seen by men. Truly I say to you, they have their reward
in full.
6 But you, when you pray, go into your inner room,
and when you have shut your door, pray to your
Father in secret, and your father who sees in secret will
repay you.
7 And when you are praying do not use meaningless
repetition, as the Gentiles do, for they suppose that
they will be heard for their many words.
8 Therefore do not be like them; for your Father knows
what you need before you ask Him.
9 Pray then in this way: "Our Father who art in Heaven,
Hallowed be thy name.
10 Thy Kingdom come.
Thy will be done.
On earth as it is in Heaven.
11 Give us this day our daily bread.
12 And forgive us our debts, as we forgive our debtors.
13 And do not lead us into temptation, but deliver us
from evil. For thine is the Kingdom and the power and
the glory, forever. Amen

Then as an adjunct, Jesus adds in verses 14 and 15, a comment to clarify in the minds of his listeners His comments in verse 12.

14. For if you forgive men for their transgression, your
Heavenly Father will also forgive you.
15. But if you do not forgive men, then your Father will
not forgive your transgressions.

I believe that Matt. 6 verses 14 and 15 are likely the cause of so many prayers not being heard or answered by God. Would Jesus have gone to all the trouble to point this out to us if "a spirit of forgiveness" was not absolutely critical to the success of our prayer life?

So if you are one of those who are holding a grudge then begin to think about the necessity of forgiveness!

Forgiveness is absolutely essential in order, according to the Lord Himself to have a successful and fulfilling prayer-life.

Now that we have covered verses 11, 14 and 15 allow me to make a few more comments about the critical nature of what is not covered in the prayer but is the preamble; verses 6, 7 and 8.

These verses are extremely instructive. Read verse 6 – "But WHEN you pray, GO INTO YOUR INNER ROOM and WHEN YOU HAVE SHUT THE DOOR, pray to your Father..."

Read it again. Jesus, our Lord tells us "where" we are to pray and it is "alone behind closed doors" and I suggest when there pray audibly to God.

Question – Have you followed these very specific instructions lately? If not please do not forget them for such is a MIGHTY SECRET to answered prayer. And if in those moments you find yourself in tears, those tears testify to your submission and devotion to Him.

Continuing in Matthew

> Matthew 21:21-22
> 21: And Jesus answered and said to them. "Truly, I say to you, if you have faith, and do not doubt, you shall not only do what was done to the fig tree, but even if you say to this mountain, 'Be taken up and cast into the sea.' It shall happen.
> 22: And all things you ask in prayer, believing, you shall receive."

Now right here the faith of the masses fails; we read those words and doubt. Such a statement by Jesus tells me how great our faith must be and reminds me how frail I am personally in exercising such a faithful faith.

References to "Pray" in Mark

We see this same comment by Jesus on faith in Mark 11:24 but in Mark also in following verse 25 is the emphasis on "forgiving others their debts" found in Matthew.

> Mark 11:24 "Therefore I say to you, all things for which you pray and ask, believe that you have them, and they shall be granted unto you."

25: "And whenever you stand praying, forgive, if you
have anything against anyone; so that your Father
also who is in Heaven may forgive your transgressions.
26: But if you do not forgive, neither will your Father
who is in Heaven forgive your transgressions."

<u>*References to "Pray" in Luke*</u>

Then in Luke 11 we find the entire chapter devoted to Jesus teaching His disciples on how to pray and the importance of being persistent in prayer.

Luke 11:5-13
5 Then he said to them, "Suppose one of you has a
friend, and he goes to him at midnight and says,
'Friend, lend me three loaves of bread, 6 because a
friend of mine on a journey has come to me, and I
have nothing to set before him.'
7 "Then the one inside answers, 'Don't bother me. The
door is already locked, and my children are with me in
bed. I can't get up and give you anything.'
8 I tell you, though he will not get up and give him the
bread because he is his friend, yet because of the
man's boldness he will get up and give him as much
as he needs.
9 "So I say to you: Ask and it will be given to you; seek
and you will find; knock and the door will be opened
to you.
10 For everyone who asks receives; he who seeks finds;
and to him who knocks, the door will be opened.
11 "Which of you fathers, if your son asks for a fish, will
give him a snake instead?
12 Or if he asks for an egg, will give him a scorpion?
13 If you then, though you are evil, know how to give
good gifts to your children, how much more will your

> 13 If you then, though you are evil, know how to give good gifts to your children, how much more will your Father in heaven give the Holy Spirit to those who ask him!" NIV
>
> Luke 18:1-8
> 18:1 Then Jesus told his disciples a parable to show them that they should always pray and not give up.
> 2 He said: "In a certain town there was a judge who neither feared God nor cared about men.
> 3 And there was a widow in that town who kept coming to him with the plea, 'Grant me justice against my adversary.'
> 4 "For some time he refused. But finally he said to himself, 'Even though I don't fear God or care about men,
> 5 yet because this widow keeps bothering me, I will see that she gets justice, so that she won't eventually wear me out with her coming!'"
> 6 And the Lord said, "Listen to what the unjust judge
> says. 7 And will not God bring about justice for his chosen ones, who cry out to him day and night? Will he keep putting them off?
> 8 I tell you, he will see that they get justice, and quickly. However, when the Son of Man comes, will he find faith on the earth?" NIV

Again in the above we see a lesson in praying with persistence. Too often I feel we offer up a brief prayer and then forget about prayer for a period, and then when the heat is on we offer up another expression of prayer and wait on the answer with doubt in our heart. See my thought on "Faith" after we look at prayer in the Gospel of John.

<u>The Gospel of John records Jesus' Priestly Prayer</u>
<u>He Prayed for the believer of the future</u>

In the Gospel of John, Chapter 17 John records the words of Jesus uttered; 26 verses in prayer to His Father God. Following are some things we can know that come out of analysis of this prayer of Jesus.

One thing we know is that Jesus prayed for you; meaning all future believers. In the first 19 verses Jesus beseeches the Father to bless the Disciples and then Jesus speaks the following words:

John 17:20-21.

> 20: "I do not ask in behalf of these alone, but for those who also believe in Me through their word.
> 21: "that they may all be one; even as Thou, Father, art in Me and I in Thee, that they may be in Us; that the world may believe that Thou didst send Me.
> 22: "And the glory which Thou hast given Me I have given them; that they may be one, just as we are one;
> 23: "I in them, and Thou in Me, that they may be perfected in unity, that the world may know that didst send Me, and did love them, even as Thou didst love Me." NASV

We know also that Jesus wants us to be filled with Joy in Him as He says in verse 13.

> John 17:13 "But now I come to Thee; and these things I speak in the world, that they may have My joy made full in themselves."

And know that Jesus wants us to win the battle with Satan in the everyday workaday world as He says in verse 15.

> John 17:15 "I do not ask Thee to take them out of the world, but to keep them from the evil one."

It is because our days are filled with the almost constant battles we fight with Satan that causes the church going masses to respond so well to any minister who will give them encouragement from God's word and reveal the love of God to them in meaningful and usable ways for everyday living.

This is the Good News!

The Gospel of Jesus Christ, which is one of hope and realization of His great love for us more than anything else.

Before we get to the Gospel of John lets analyze where Faith fits in?

Jesus taught that faith and believing are the essence of prayer with no room for doubt. Without faith prayer is rendered powerless. If on many occasions we mostly see no power in our prayers might we have a problem with faith and believing?

In response to the faith of a believer it is my belief that God is now actively loving each and every one, of His children and as He does I do not believe He is busy devising another way to punish us for our latest sin.

Rather God is saying to us, "Come unto me my child. Show me your faith. You are living a life of violation." He literally pleads with us to avoid Satan's ways. The punishment that does come from our disobedience arrives through the immutable "consequences of sin" laws of the creation. For an action there is a reaction. Such is the rule of science, just as it is in every day living and just as it was from the beginning of time. God ordained it. If you violate His spiritual laws, there will be consequences.

We just do not know when, how or what! Sometimes it is immediate, at other times it comes over a lifetime of sad remembrance of our failure.

So once again, of this I believe, under His covenant of Grace, God is not sitting on His throne waiting to give the; "PUNISH" order as soon as we disobey. Rather the results of sin will be along in time and I believe God takes no pleasure in our suffering as a consequence of our sin. Sin causes suffering; sometimes it is now, sometimes it is later and sometimes it is ongoing."

Sin will not be denied! The wages of sin is "death," BUT the GIFT of God is eternal life through Jesus Christ, God's Son. God calls us to have faith and follow Him.

Since in the creation event God gave us total choice as to our demeanor and since we are faced on the one hand with the temptations put up by Satan and on the other hand the joy of knowing God through Jesus Christ it is the nature of man to want both. As a result we live our lives with a giant "cross-pull" on our choices day by day.

It is how we manage this cross-pull that ultimately determines our destiny. It is our choice; live life with self in control or live life with Christ in control. Through Jesus Christ God offers His love to guide us in living.

Let's examine, through logic, the Love of God.

CHAPTER 13

Seeing God's Love

To me an engineer and acquainted (somewhat) with the physical laws of the universe it is evident to me in the Created Universe that God the creator is infinitely logical. However there are some who contradict this position; but in support of my belief I give you a quote from Dr. Hugh Ross, PHD in Astronomy on this subject to reinforce my position.

From Dr. Hugh Ross we find the following statement.

> "Some people argue that applying logic to religion is false or misleading. They insist that ultimate truth comes only through some type of non-rational intuition. Their argument betrays them, however, because in arguing against logic they must first presuppose the laws of logic to attempt a refutation. To do so is, of course, self-contradictory. As Christian apologists Norman Geisler and Ronald Brooks point out, "Even those who claim, 'Logic does not apply to God,' use logic in that very statement."

> To divorce oneself from the self-evident laws of thought when it comes to ultimate reality is to resign oneself to irrationality. Netland explains a price too great for most people to pay because it requires the "forfeiture of the possibility of meaningful affirmation or statement about anything at all—including statements about the religious ultimate. One who rejects the principle of non-contradiction is reduced to utter silence, for he or she has abandoned a necessary condition for any coherent or meaningful position whatsoever."

Thus, I believe that mere man can come a bit closer to knowing and understanding God if we approach God and His purposes using an analysis process of Biblically based logic.

Most all humans have at one time or another looked at the stars in the still of the night and wondered; wondered about space, stars, tremendous size of the solar system, the immensity of our galaxy and the vastness of space.

I remember a poem I learned as a teenager named "Stars" by Sara Teasdale.

Poem lyrics of Stars by Sarah Teasdale.

Alone in the night
On a dark hill
With pines around me
Spicy and still,

And a heaven full of stars
Over my head,
White and topaz
And misty red;

Myriads with beating
Hearts of fire
That aeons
Cannot vex or tire;

Up the dome of heaven
Like a great hill,
I watch them marching
Stately and still,

And I know that I
Am honored to be

Witness
Of so much majesty.

Human reflection on our origins is natural.

The questions we all ask are-
Where did it all come from? Why is it here? Why are we here? Why am I here? Is there a Creator God?

If there is a Creator God does He/She/It care about me?

Following these questions from deep within we wonder; what is our ultimate individual fate to be?

If there is a God will I be accepted by Him when I die?

If such a Supreme Being exists and Heaven is a real place, will I be allowed entrance into Heaven?

This natural inquisitiveness seems to be psychologically and perhaps biologically contained in our beings. It seems deep inside each heart and mind there is a longing to know our creator. Some even say there is a God shaped vacuum in the heart of man that can only be filled by God.

A few years ago I wrote a poem containing that idea.

The God Space

There is a God shaped vacuum in the soul of
everyman
We can stuff it, cram it, fill it with everything we can
But it will still be empty, because don't you see,
It belongs to God only, it doesn't belong to me.

We can curse it or deny it but there it will remain,
That God shaped vacuum will always be the same.
It will still be empty, because don't you see,
It belongs to God alone, it doesn't belong to me.

Pack it with riches and glory and act satisfied,
But it will still be empty, for God will not be denied.
We can ignore it or forget it, but it does not go a way;
It will always be there just waiting for that day.

There is a God shaped vacuum in the soul of
everyone,
Waiting to be filled by God's only Son.
And our God is waiting to fill it at our invitation,
To be filled by Christ Jesus, sealing our salvation.
Emmitt J. Nelson 1996

We certainly know that man strives to learn more of the answers to the above questions about the universe through studies and research in many areas of science, physics, astrophysics, astronomy and mathematics.

NASA and others now believe the Earth orbiting Hubble Telescope has come close to seeing (taken a picture of) the edge of the universe.

> NASA's Next Generation Space Telescope, scheduled to be launched in 2007, may provide definitive answers. Its lens will be three times bigger than Hubble's, and it will be able to see objects 20 to 25 times fainter, according to Ed Weiler, head of NASA's office of space science.

> Some astronomers hope it will surely allow them to view the very edge of the universe, the "dark zone" beyond which there are no stars or galaxies.
>
> "If the Next Generation telescope doesn't see the edge, I don't know what would," said Weiler.

Scientists, through analysis using the laws of Physics now believe they have determined that "it" all began in the distant past with a creation event they have come to call "The Big Bang."

In other words their belief is, as far as the universe is concerned, that originally there was nothing of a "time, matter, space" dimension. Then from a single infinitesimally tiny point, called a "singularity point," the creation of the universe began, suddenly and explosively.

This belief implies that, just as the Bible states, what we now see all began from nothing. From that explosive event what we know of today as "The Universe" was created. This "event" corresponds to the phrase "In the beginning God created..." the Bible opens with.

God Given Order of Creation Events

Found in the Bible in the first chapter of the book of Genesis the creation events are listed in a specific order. Dr. Hugh Ross, noted Astrophysicist, tells us that there are 18 creation events listed and they are given in an exact and scientifically required order when one views them in light of the known laws of modern physics. Dr. Ross adds that the odds of any writer in ancient times compiling such an exact chronologically accurate list matching the laws of modern physics would be billions of billions to one. Thus he concludes that even the author of Genesis was given the order of the creation events by God through inspiration.

Though some humans are believers, some agnostics, some skeptics, some seeking, others atheists, many who are "creation thinkers" argue that the very fact that we ponder all these things is proof we are but created beings. These conclude that there is a Supreme Power or Intelligence (commonly known as God) that set in motion the seasons and goings and comings of planetary events including those events on this planet we call Earth that are distinctly human in nature. My beliefs belong in this latter group and my remarks are so structured.

Thus I believe there is a logic set growing out of modern science and technology that adequately proves the omniscience of God. That God is all knowing and is concerned about us as the Bible states in the Gospel of Matthew.

> Matt 10:29 Are not two sparrows sold for a penny? Yet not one of them will fall to the ground apart from the will of your Father.
> 30 And even the very hairs of your head are all numbered.

> 31 So don't be afraid; you are worth more than many sparrows. NIV

Note the statement that God has numbered the hairs on our head.

We ask "How can this be?"

There are around seven billion humans on earth.

How can God know the numbers of hairs on the head of each; further why would God care about the hair on our head?

On the plausibility of God knowing this seemingly meaningless detail let me point out that in our day (2006) with the expansion of computer memory technology over the past 20 years, the development of electronic memory capability has been vast. Imagine a small thin silicon chip the size of a thumbnail and realize that God's creation, Man, has learned how to store the equivalent of a library of information in this tiny chip.

If Man can achieve such amazing technical progress in memory with our intellectual limitations who are we to question God on how much information He has the capability to keep track of or have infinite detail on?

So as we ponder this in wonderment, most of us stop in shadow of the "awe" that comes from such deep thinking. We say "wow" and move on. Some get mentally bogged down just thinking about such, so had rather not think about it at all.

Though all wonder, only a minority of humans venture very far into the realms of thought on the "why of our being?"

As individuals we accept God, deny Him or simply put off any decision or ignore the subject. Those who deny God typically will build a personal body of logic that justifies their stance; often based on the concept of "I am as good as the rest so if there is a Heaven I will get there when I die. If there is no Heaven then it does not matter." Or I have heard it said in defense of an Agnostic position that just because what we see seems so logical does not mean that there is a God that created it.

Countering these, many of those who believe in God have an inbuilt intuition that He exists (the God shaped vacuum if you will) and accept Him on faith, live accordingly but also devote little, if any, thought to the subject of creation and the logic of God and His love.

In historical review it seems there have always been spiritual leaders in all races of peoples who have created a theological logic set that gives explanation to these questions of the how and why of their origin.

These bodies of theological logic, while perhaps not always simple, on the surface are generally easily understood and accepted by the mass of people. Thus the mass of individual curiosity is salved.

But, perchance, even if one wishes to, on one's on accord venture more deeply into these subjects of "origins" it is typical that few others of their acquaintances will want to know very much of that individual's ponderings; "Too deep for me," they say or when discussed their eyes glaze over and they change the subject or simply walk away.

Of the many "origins theologies in the world" there is one that in and of itself is so logical that for millions it becomes the preferred explanation of "why we are here."

One could call it the "Judeo-Christian" origins, but I prefer to call it the "Christian belief system." Like no other man recorded logic, it is based on the concept of "God's love" for man and His willingness to forgive our sinfulness.

Here, right away we need to define in the English language the type of "Love" referenced. In the Greek language this form of Love is called Agape. It is not the carnal love of sexual fulfillment. Further it is not the warm love of family.

Agape is defined as that love that is on the highest of social planes of thought; nothing carnal or selfish, but a pure love that has at its very base a desire for the greater good to befall all peoples. By its very nature this love gives priority to others before self.

As all readers will likely know, the foundational work that underpins the Judeo-Christian belief system is the Bible; a collection of 66 writings or books of ancient origins, formally selected to be included in the Bible on the basis of the harmony (cultural, historical and spiritual) of the collective message found in these individually compiled books.

The central figure in the Bible is Jesus Christ. To the believing Jew He is the Messiah. To all others who believe, the Bible is the inspired word of God telling of the life, death and resurrection of Jesus Christ is the definitive poof of God's love for created man. In John 3 we find the following:

> John 3:16 "For God so loved the world that he gave his one and only Son, that whoever believes in him shall not perish but have eternal life.
> 17 For God did not send his Son into the world to condemn the world, but to save the world through Him.
> 18 Whoever believes in Him is not condemned, but whoever does not believe stands condemned already because he has not believed in the name of God's
> one and only Son. 19 This is the verdict: Light has come into the world, but men loved darkness instead of light because their deeds were evil.
> 20 Everyone who does evil hates the light, and will not come into the light for fear that his deeds will be exposed.

> 21 But whoever lives by the truth comes into the light, so that it may be seen plainly that what he has done has been done through God." NIV

Of the 66 books in the Bible many believe that the Fourth Gospel, The Gospel of John, is the foundational if not pivotal book that supports and lends indisputable credibility to the Christian belief system being based on love.

Written by John, the Apostle, an eye witnesses to Jesus' death on the cross and His subsequent resurrection; the same John who heard Jesus ask Peter three times, "Do you love me?" John 21, 15-17.

Also, this is the same John who is called by many the "Love Apostle" because of the 73 references to "love" in his five contributions to the 66 books of the Bible. (The Gospel of John; 1st, 2nd & 3rd John and Revelation.) Especially in 1st John one finds references to "love" 35 times; more than any other book in the New Testament.

My contention is that the reason God created the Universe and then man was for fellowship through Agape Love; God wanted love to come into existence, to be freely demonstrated; to be reciprocated; to be shared, to be felt, to be an inspiration; to man and to all of Heaven's population.

Thus in order to demonstrate love, I believe the creation of Man was God's focal point of creation. It is obvious if God was going to create Man, He first had to create a place for man to live; thus the universe and the planetary systems.

Yes, I believe the ultimate purpose of God's creation of the Universe was to provide man a dwelling place in the space-time dimension.

This is logical.

How can I say all this?

Allow me to do another logic check. This will take a few pages.

If we can establish through logic that it is true that God created man for Love and Fellowship, it will assist in understanding the nature of God's love.

First a simple question; "Can we possibly understand God's love?"

"Can we define God's love in such a way as to reveal God's purpose to the masses of peoples flowing from this creation event?"

In order to approach this subject there are a number of problems that need to be addressed.

CHAPTER 14

Defining God's Love

The Language Problem

Attempting to communicate on such a spiritually deep and intellectually challenging subject requires the use of language which in and of itself is limiting. Compiling words to express meaning, and a convincing logic to explore God is fraught with the inadequacies of language. But nonetheless if you are interested in following the composed words we shall try.

I say "we" for I write and you read; thus interdependency exists between us.

The first book of the Bible begins with these words; "In the beginning God created the Heavens and the Earth." Genesis 1:1. It is such a simple statement but as simple as it is, this statement has been and likely will be the center of controversy for all time.

The Big Bang

The Creation Word:

Ponder the word "create" for a moment. The word itself implies the passing of time. Time was required for creation to take place. The time consumed would have been of measurable length as modern Astrophysicists claim. An interesting attribute of time is that it is relative. A long time in one sense can be a very short time in another. While time was required for creation to occur it does not really matter how much time was used until a "time dependent" intelligent creature was also created.

Many wish to argue the first 20 verses of the Book of Genesis is literally 7 days as we now measure them as planetary events 24 hours in length. This argument is offered by advocates to test the belief system of those who through logic see that it really does not matter just exactly how long it took for the earth to become what it now is, from the finite point as time began when the "Big Bang" (creation) occurred.

Others point out that if God has the power to create, He can do it in anyway He wishes. But some ask, what about this business of carbon dating that indicates billions of years have passed since certain types of rock were formed?

On the subject of the "7 days of 24 hours" creation I prefer to think this way. If God has this creative power in the first place, might He also have the power to create "old rocks" or are we going to limit the creating God in such a way that He can only create "new rocks?"

The latter is not logical! The former (7 epochs of unknown length) fits my scientifically inclined mind.

As far as we know only animate beings have instincts or intelligence and are time aware. Items such as water, rocks and dirt are not time aware but in fact they do have a cellular functionality that is time dependent for in these in-animate objects there are atoms and electrons and these are in a constant state of movement at set frequencies.

Have you ever considered that everything in the universe is alive at the cellular level; nothing excluded. Even the decaying body of an animal is alive at the cellular level. Not alive as in a functioning animal created by God but nonetheless alive in the decaying process.

Rocks and such are not considered "life" by modern scientists. But in fact they are alive at the cellular level. However the things we call "living things" such as trees, moss, grass, flora and fauna have a time dependency though one could argue they are not aware of time in any intellectual sense. Me; I am not so sure about that!

Where did God come from?

Where does God fit into this time puzzle?

Is God getting older?

The Bible reveals that God is not time dependent and exists outside the created space-time dimensions. God existed prior to His creation of what we humans know about and see. God refers to self in the Bible as "I Am." This term infers that God was, is and will be; in other words ageless.

For God to create the universe He pre-existed the universe. Judaic Christian thought reveals God as the great center of all that was, is and all that will be. This is inferred when in Exodus God gives himself the name of "I AM." "I AM" is a present tense name. "I AM," in the "present tense" yesterday, today and tomorrow. Exodus 3:13-14.

> Ex 3:13 Moses said to God, "Suppose I go to the Israelites and say to them, 'The God of your fathers has sent me to you,' and they ask me, 'What is his name?' Then what shall I tell them?"
> 14 God said to Moses, "I AM WHO I AM. This is what you are to say to the Israelites: 'I AM has sent me to you.'"
> NIV

While God does manifest Himself within the time-space universe continuum He created, God in fact also exists outside the time-space limited universe.

Time Space Limitations of Man

Think about the following concept. God created man and put him literally in a box. The walls of the box are not finite but infinite as far as man is concerned. Our box is defined by our lifetime and the immense size of the universe thus our walls of confinement are made of time and we are confined by our limited life span.

While in Genesis early man often lived in excess of 900 years we also know from Genesis that after Noah, God limited the life span of man to 120 years.

> Gen 6:3 Then the LORD said, "My Spirit will not contend with man forever, for he is mortal; his days will be a hundred and twenty years." NIV

In 120 years a man could hardly travel (using currently known means of travel) to the next star let alone to the next galaxy or to ends of the universe. We are in fact created beings contained in a time and space box. There is no danger of us escaping our space time box even if we so wanted. Given the modern technology of space travel we are still confined. According to Einstein's Theory of Relativity it is impossible for an object of weight to travel at the speed of light because it would become infinitely massive in weight.

It is because of this speed of light that we have learned as much as we have about the universe. Light travels at the speed of 186,000 miles per second.

With 3600 seconds in an hour light travels at the amazing speed of 669,600,000 miles per hour.

In a day light travels an amazing 16,070,400,000 miles.

In a year light travels 5,865,696,000,000 miles; or almost 6 million million miles; a distance known as a light year.

Our Galaxy is estimated to be 100,000 light years in diameter. If man was technologically able to travel as fast as light it would take 833 life spans of 120 years simply to travel across the diameter of our Milky Way Galaxy.

Armed with this "gee whiz" knowledge it seems to me that the universe is too large for the mind of man to comprehend. For instance in the Milky Way Galaxy there are near 200 billion stars the size of our Sun. Further there are an estimated 250 billion galaxies like ours in the universe.

So what does all this time distance have to do with us?

It makes us infinitesimally tiny in relation to the grander scale of the universe and further emphasizes the question man asks of "Why?" Why a universe, why a galaxy, why an earth, why man?

And I propose this same scale and our lack of an ability to relate to it or in fact comprehend the vastness of it, in and of itself, proves the existence of God. It is easy to see that our natural environment is uniquely technologically advanced. I say this and argue technologically advanced even with out a single contribution by man. The creation, the physics of it all, the fact that it is in gravitational balance and living creatures including man in highly complex bodies proves to me beyond a shadow of a doubt that God is behind it all.

As I say this I recognize there are some who disagree and that is OK.

The Time Problem:

What is required for "time" to be a reality?

The answer to this is "something that is time dependant."

In other words if there is nothing physical, no time can exist. Only in the instant of creation of the universe (something physical became) did time as a dimension come into being.

Without "something" nothing can "change." And we know "change" is a time dependent process.

As far as we know only God and His creation, man, are "intellectually" aware of the passing of time. This statement by using the word "intellectually" places the animal kingdom, sans man, with the capacity to be "biologically" aware of time and the passing thereof but not cognitively so. But in fact we do not know about animals as far as cognitive skills are concerned.

It is obvious to the observer that both domestic and wild animals, birds and fishes are aware of the passing of time and will follow instincts in migration, feeding and mating. Some of this, such as mating, can be termed "biological time related awareness."

Weather and seasons do result in biological change over time in both flora and fauna but the intellectual ability to count days, prepare a calendar and track the heavenly bodies across the universe belongs entirely in the human race. (As far as we know.)

The Final Problem: "Why Man"

Why, in the creation act, did God create man?

In direct words (God would say audibly so all would have no doubt "I created man for love.") we do not know, but from Biblical study we can reach a plausible answer. We can first notice that a plural God created man in "Our image" or likeness.

> Gen 1:26 Then God said, "Let 'us' make man in 'our' image, in 'our' likeness, and let them rule over the fish of the sea and the birds of the air, over the livestock,

> over all the earth, and over all the creatures that move along the ground."
> 27 So God created man in his own image, in the image of God he created him; male and female he created them. NIV

I believe this "likeness" would surely be a "spiritual" likeness, but some say a physical likeness as well, but how can God who is Omnipotent create a finite figure in His Omnipresent image. Well He could create a finite being that looks like a "spirit" being. While this statement can imply a definite Godly acceptance of the appearance of man; something to be admired, as to look on a likeness of oneself can be sometimes pleasurable; Genesis 1:26 very definitely implies at least a spiritual likeness.

Adam, the first man, early in his God given life, failed the Creator and did not live up to God's Holy expectations. An obvious question arises. If God is all intelligent why could He not create man to have a higher standard of values and morals? This too is answerable through the defining of God's love. So allow me to continue.

Implied in Genesis is God's purpose of "fellowship with man."

> Gen 3:8 Then the man and his wife heard the sound of the LORD God as he was walking in the garden in the cool of the day, and they hid from the LORD God among the trees of the garden.
> 9 But the LORD God called to the man, "Where are you?"

> 10 Man answered, "I heard you in the garden, and I
> was afraid because I was naked; so I hid."
> 11 And God said, "Who told you that you were naked?
> Have you eaten from the tree that I commanded you
> not to eat from?" NIV

Verse 8 implies that God walked in the Garden of Eden in the cool of the day for pleasure and by implication to fellowship with Adam and Eve. In verse 9 God called out to Adam this question; "Where are you." In other words Adam was not physically or relationally where God expected to find him.

Right away we hear Adam reply; "...I was afraid...so I hid...;" a relationship based answer. Afraid because Adam knew he had failed God.

Though this question of "Where are you?" is Biblically recorded creation history it has an immediate and present application. In fact, as far as God is concerned the question is eternal and applies to all people in the here and now.

Through Bible Study we know where God wants us to be spiritually; that being in close fellowship with Him. So as we live day by day, minute by minute, and listen to God, He is asking each "Where are you?"

"Where are you," in your efforts to live a God centered life.

"Where are you," in our relationship, you and I?

"Where are you," in your relationship with your fellow man?

"Where are you," in living up to the "Great Commandment?"

> Matt 22:36 "Teacher, which is the greatest commandment in the Law?"
> 37 Jesus replied: "'Love the Lord your God with all your heart and with all your soul and with all your mind.'
> 38 This is the first and greatest commandment. 39 And the second is like it: 'Love your neighbor as yourself.' NIV

After this "Where are you?" question from God to Adam, we learn that God's created man had fallen to the temptation of the Serpent. We could try to imagine how this failure made God feel. First we can visualize His great disappointment. What to do about the failure was obvious under the circumstances.

In view of other possibilities that Man could violate God's rules He immediately knew Man had to be expelled from the Garden of Eden for the Garden also had a plant that yielded fruit if eaten would give man "eternal life" in the flesh.

> Gen 3:22 And the LORD God said, "The man has now become like one of us, knowing good and evil. He must not be allowed to reach out his hand and take also from the tree of life and eat, and live forever." 23 So the LORD God banished him from the Garden of Eden to work the ground from which he had been taken. NIV

Notice something in the above verses. God took away the potential for man to have something He later gave back.

He took away the possibility that man eat of the Tree of Life and live forever. Yet, it seems "eternal life" is exactly what God later gave us through Jesus Christ. Of interest is that God did not forbid Adam to eat from The Tree of Life initially but only after he ate of the fruit of The Tree of Knowledge of Good and Evil.

Again, the immediate question is; "Why?"

There is logic that may explain this point. If man had eaten of the Tree of Life having first eaten of the Tree of Knowledge of Good and Evil; then man would live forever in the flesh where evil and corruption could abound and there would be a host of Satan disciples eternally alive on earth. God knew that if evil were released in such a fashion there would be no chance for "love" to survive. The world would become a growing boiling caldron of evil eternal upon the earth.

All know that even in this day it is a mighty ongoing struggle for love to oppose evil and terrorism among our cultures in the 21st Century.

God knew the only way to wage some control over evil on the earth was to control the life span of man. Thus no man could forever plague the earth with his own brand of eternal evil presence. Everyone must die in the flesh and only the spirit lives on; the evil spirits to be cast out and the saved spirits to Heaven.

But, as it happened we are promised eternal life for our souls. The saved souls of believers will live in the spiritual realm, where God controls the environment and evil will not be allowed co-exist with us in Heaven.

"Commandment" Guidance from God

Later in the book of Exodus God gives to Man the 10 Commandments. The first four of these commandments deals with Man's relationship with God; instructing Man on how to live in relationship with his Creator. These four commandments are very instructive as we attempt to find God's purpose in creating Man. The 10 Commandments:

> Ex 20:1 Then God issued this edict:
> 2 "I am Jehovah your God who liberated you from your slavery in Egypt.
>
> **First Commandment**
> 3 "You may worship no other god than me.
>
> **Second Commandment**
> 4 "You shall not make yourselves any idols: no images of animals, birds, or fish.
> 5 You must never bow or worship it in any way; for I, the Lord your God, am very possessive. I will not share your affection with any other god! "And when I punish people for their sins, the punishment continues upon

the children, grandchildren, and great-grandchildren
of those who hate me;
6 but I lavish my love upon thousands of those who
love me and obey my commandments.

Third Commandment

7 "You shall not use the name of Jehovah your God
irreverently, nor use it to swear to a falsehood. You will
not escape punishment if you do.

Fourth Commandment

8 "Remember to observe the Sabbath as a holy day.
9 Six days a week are for your daily duties and your
regular work,
10 but the seventh day is a day of Sabbath rest before
the Lord your God. On that day you are to do no work
of any kind, nor shall your son, daughter, or slaves-
whether men or women-or your cattle or your house
guests.
11 For in six days the Lord made the heaven, earth,
and sea, and everything in them, and rested the
seventh day; so he blessed the Sabbath day and set it
aside for rest.

Last Six Commandments

12 "Honor your father and mother, that you may have
a long, good life in the land the Lord your God will
give you.
13 "You must not murder.
14 "You must not commit adultery.
15 "You must not steal.
16 "You must not lie.
17 "You must not be envious of your neighbor's house,
or want to sleep with his wife, or want to own his
slaves, oxen, donkeys, or anything else he has." TLB

Ten into Two

Jesus summed the 10 Commandments into two when asked to name the greatest commandment. He responded with a singular emphasis on love. In doing so God again introduced to the believer the notion that what God really wants of and from man is love.

> Matt 22:35 One of them, an expert in the law, tested him with this question:
> 36 "Teacher, which is the greatest commandment in the Law?"
> 37 Jesus replied: "'Love the Lord your God with all your heart and with all your soul and with all your mind.'
> 38 This is the first and greatest commandment.
> 39 And the second is like it: 'Love your neighbor as yourself.'
> 40 All the Law and the Prophets hang on these two commandments." NIV

In Verse 37 Jesus covers the first four commandments; and in verse 39 He covered the last six commandments. Note the central theme of love. This examination gives tremendous insight into the why of creation.

Again, I believe that God's love expressed through Jesus Christ is the cornerstone of the Bible message from God and pull primarily from the New Testament scriptures to explore this belief.

CHAPTER 15

LOVE; God's and Our Own

How does one go about understanding the enormity of God's love for His creation man? I have borrowed most of this chapter from my book, "The Fruit of the Spirit."

To answer this question my approach will be to again use logic as we explore scripture words that from that from the original New Testament Greek referred to Agape love; or "the love of God." The English word "love" appears 550 times in the New International version of the Bible with 232 uses appearing in the New Testament which as I say was originally written in Greek. But only a portion of these 232 are used as the Greek Agape love meaning to love in a "social or moral sense."

Consider that the Spirit fruit of "love" (Galatians 5:22-23) should be spiritually viewed as both internal and external.

> Gal 5:22 But the fruit of the Spirit is love, joy, peace, patience, kindness, goodness, faithfulness,

> 23 gentleness and self-control. Against such things there is no law. NIV

Love first came to man externally in the sense that God first loved us. In the beginning "God so loved the world..." John 3:16. Then second this love becomes internal when we accept God's love through Jesus Christ.

> John 3:16 "For God so loved the world that he gave his one and only Son, that whoever believes in him shall not perish but have eternal life. (NIV)

Jesus, in the greatest commandment (Matt. 22:37) told us directly and unequivocally that we are to "Love the Lord your God...", and further made it very clear that it is a healthy human condition that we love ourselves. (And that such "self love" is expected by God) Then in the same verses Jesus tells us to "love our neighbor as ourselves." Second commandment to the "...first and greatest commandment" is to "love your neighbor as yourselves"

> Matthew 22:37 Jesus replied: '"Love the Lord your God with all your heart and with all your soul and with all your mind.
> 38. This is the first and greatest commandment.
> 39. And the second is like it: 'Love your neighbor as yourself.'" (NIV)

The "love our neighbor" carries this Love external again, but this time built on the internal, in that we must learn to love others, even the unlovable. See Luke 6.

> Luke 6:32 "If you love those who love you, what credit is that to you? Even 'sinners' love those who love them. 33 And if you do good to those who are good to you, what credit is that to you? Even 'sinners' do that. NIV

<u>It is Man's Option</u>

As previously pointed out, in creating Man for fellowship and love, God revealed the enormity and totality of His love by giving His creation, Man the total and absolute option to reject the Creator.

Our free will as created beings is total and complete. There are no physical or other unalterable pre-disposed God created constraints placed upon our free will. Oh, there are stated moral constraints enough beginning with the 10 Commandments, but it is only through our free will that we exercise any restraint and that by our own volition and will.

In my view these facts define the enormity of God's love toward us. With this broad latitude of moral freedom it was a given that some men would fall away, would travel the lower road. They would travel this lower road knowing full well that the course of action they were taking was contrary to God's wishes for them.

This being the case, when that one individual took the high road and chose God's way, there was much joy in Heaven.

> Luke 15:7 Jesus speaking -
> 7 I tell you that in the same way there will be more rejoicing in heaven over one sinner who repents than over ninety-nine righteous persons who do not need to repent. NIV

Again remember as the foundation to developing love for others we must learn to forgive others, as challenged in The Lord's Prayer, "Forgive us our trespasses as we forgive those who trespass against us." Mathew 6:12.

When we forgive we are immolating God for God is the preeminent forgiver. When God revealed Himself to Moses as recorded first in Exodus Chapter 34 we find the following statement by God.

> Ex 34:6 And the LORD passed before him and proclaimed, "The LORD, the LORD God, merciful and gracious, longsuffering, and abounding in goodness and truth,
> 7 keeping mercy for thousands, forgiving iniquity and transgression and sin..." NKJV

Then again we find God's forgiveness revealed in the 2nd Chapter of Acts.

> Acts 2:38 Peter replied, "Repent and be baptized, every one of you, in the name of Jesus Christ for the forgiveness of your sins. And you will receive the gift of the Holy Spirit.

> 39 The promise is for you and your children and for all who are far off - for all whom the Lord our God will call." NIV

When we accept Christ and become a believer, God forgives us our past sin and in the same instant sends the Holy Spirit to dwell in our hearts. We then with the help of the Holy Spirit we are empowered to learn to forgive others as we begin our work of developing the first spirit fruit of "love."

It is in the Old Testament that we find the description of how we should love God in Deuteronomy 6:5. I propose the description of how wee should love God is also in critical order as given; heart is first, soul is second, then strength.

> Deuteronomy 6:5 - Love the LORD your God with all your heart and with all your soul and with all your strength. **(NIV)**

Since our "soul" is directly connected to the desires and purposes of our "heart" it is logical that "heart" must be the center of our ability to "love." Our loving creator God comes first as we show this priority in accepting Him into our "heart." With this "heart" acceptance we in effect give our God given "soul" back to God.

The word "soul" is used in the Bible to portray that personal and uniquely ours, spirit who is eternal within each of us. Our souls are in fact our eternal lives; locked for a time in the body of a visiting sojourner upon the planet earth.

So the Deuteronomy 6:5 message urges us to apply internal and external energies, in the eternal sense to loving God in an active sense. After all it was God who created us with a "living soul."

> Genesis 2:7 And the LORD God formed man of the dust of the ground, and breathed into his nostrils the breath of life; and man became a living soul. (KJV)

Just as it is clear that God created man with a "living soul" it is also clear from the scripture in the Gospels that Jesus was sent to dwell on earth to provide us eternal life by saving our "souls" through His sacrifice.

> Luke 19:10 For the Son of Man came to seek and to save what was lost." (NIV)
>
> Mark 8:35 For whoever wants to save his life will lose it, but whoever loses his life for me and for the gospel will save it.
> 36) What good is it for a man to gain the whole world, yet forfeit his soul?
> 37) Or what can a man give in exchange for his soul? (NIV)
>
> John 3:17 For God did not send his Son into the world to condemn the world, but to save the world through him. (NIV)

Therefore, God's clear priority in our lives is that we devote this life given to us by God back to Him. Not for His sake but for our souls' sake and then our life's sake as we live in this world. So here we hear God command us to love Him for His sake and for our own good as well.

Once "we want" to give our 'heart and soul' back to God, as the scripture urges us to do, we find the scripture also tells us how to do this. We should give it -- "...with all your...." "With all your" heart, "with all your" soul and "with all your" strength. I am altering the original in the following verse. Deuteronomy 6:5 "Love the Lord your God..." - first "with all your heart" then "with all your soul..." and finally "with all your strength...."

Why the words "...with all your...?"

Because God knows that unless we are very careful, the "things of the world" will dilute our zeal in loving God. Then our diluted zeal produces diluted blessings that result from our diluted obedience to Him.

Hence we should not forget the words --"...with all your..."-- for therein lies one of the great secrets of the Christian life.

Our complete loving of God will yield a completely fulfilled life. Fulfilled with "...the fruit of the Spirit..." and a lot of other blessings that come to us as we do what God asks of us.

Jesus, in the Sermon on the Mount, in Matthew 5 and 6, gives us a glimpse of the proper arranging of life's priorities. In this sermon Jesus addresses man's concern for material things and man's worries about life.

See Matthew 6:25-34. Jesus sums up by speaking these words in verses 33 and 34.

> "But seek first His Kingdom and His righteousness and all these things will be given to you as well. Therefore do not worry about tomorrow, for tomorrow will worry about itself. Each day has enough trouble of its own." (NIV)

We could easily place the words "...with all your...heart, soul, strength..." right in the middle of the above words of Jesus. For instance - "But seek ye first, 'with. all. your. heart. soul. strength' the Kingdom."

With such a placement of words reflecting life priorities we would portray the depth of what Jesus was attempting to impart to us in the way of setting priorities as we live our life here on earth.

The Spirit Comes

Through Jesus all are invited to salvation's door, to open it when we hear Jesus' "knock and His voice." We are invited in, to listen and accept the terms of salvation.

The subject of recognizing the voice of Jesus' is found again in John, Chapter 10. On this occasion Jesus is speaking to a group of Jewish Pharisees. Jesus is telling them of His role as the Good Shepherd.

John 10:1 "Truly, truly, I say to you, he who does not
enter by the door into the fold of the sheep, but
climbs up some other way, he is a thief and a
robber.
2 "But he who enters by the door is a shepherd of
the sheep.
3 "To him the doorkeeper opens, and the sheep
hear his voice, and he calls his own sheep by
name, and leads them out.
4 "When he puts forth all his own, he goes before
them, and the sheep follow him because they
know "his voice."
5 "And a stranger they simply will not follow, but will
flee from him, because they do not know the voice
of strangers."
9 "I am the door; if anyone enters through Me, he
shall be saved, and shall go in and out, and find
pasture.
10 "The thief comes only to steal, and kill, and
destroy; I came that they might have life, and
might have it abundantly.
11 "I am the good shepherd; the good shepherd
lays down His life for the sheep.
14 "I am the good shepherd; and I know My own,
and My own know Me,
15 even as the Father knows Me and I know the
Father; and I lay down My life for the sheep.
16 "And I have other sheep, which are not of this
fold; I must bring them also, and they shall hear My
voice; and they shall become one flock with one
shepherd.

The 16th verse is a reference to the non-Jewish peoples who were to be admitted into the family of

God through Jesus' sacrifice on the cross: specifically the Gentiles.

Jesus also reminds us, that for our salvation we must publicly express our commitment to Jesus as our Savior and Lord.

> Matthew 10:32 "Whoever acknowledges me before men, I will also acknowledge him before my Father in heaven.
> 33. But whoever disowns me before men, I will disown him before my Father in heaven." (NIV)

A crucial thing happens when "we give our heart" to God through Jesus. This crucial "happening" must precede our attempts to communicate with God through our own efforts. We are to place our trust in Christ and it, "the happening," will occur automatically. For you see when we give our hearts to God through Jesus, God gives us back "the Holy Spirit."

While God promises us the Holy Spirit upon believing in Christ, in a manner of thinking it is a gift therefore it must be accepted. A gift unaccepted is not a gift at all, but a "slam" to the individual offering the gift. Please do not "slam" God.

Claim Christ and accept His gift unconditionally!

The truth is, if we fail to follow through in living up to our commitment to Christ then the "gift" falls by the wayside as not accepted and thus not usable.

If we are truly saved the Holy Spirit will be tending our hearts and reminding us of our original commitment until we die. Literally the Spirit becomes "the hound of Heaven." God wants us to be all we can be, and we can only be so if we follow Him and allow Him to lead us. Our own gift of the Holy Spirit will always be reminding us of this. Another scripture on this "gift" concept is:

> Acts 2:28 Peter replied, "Repent and be baptized, every one of you, in the name of Jesus Christ for the forgiveness of your sins. And you will receive the gift of the Holy Spirit." NIV

The operative word in the above verse is "repent." This simply means that we must look on our past life and see the sin, admit the sin and feel true sorrow for the sin and make an agreement with God that we will in the future be committed to Him through Jesus Christ.

The above paragraph describes the process of being "born again;" or born of the Spirit. Remember the gift referenced is that very "Holy Spirit" that will ultimately assist us as we work to produce those fruit of Galatians 5:22-23. What if we work very hard and then fail? Is "close" good enough when we strive to live out our life as Christians?

My belief is this. Once we cross the sin barrier between God and Man, which we cross when we accept Christ as our Savior then the truth is, when our total life is viewed, "close to sinless is about all we can be."

Before we accept Christ we are far, far away from a sinless life for we are living in un-forgiven sin. Even honest and good people with sins of small proportions are nonetheless in sin as far as God is concerned. Romans 3:23 tells us this.

> "...FOR ALL HAVE SINNED AND COME SHORT OF THE GLORY OF GOD..." NIV

The reason we should accept Christ is quite simple. God created us; God commanded us to "Love God" and then gave us the path to Him: Jesus Christ who is our sin sacrifice. Our, the creation's role, is to "accept" God's, the Creator's plan, not argue with Him about it.

Good people can live good lives, but a good life is not what God wants first. He wants our heart first, and then His Spirit will be our helper in living a good life. Through Christ, God provides forgiveness for our failing. In living a good life apart from God one has only the not so small problem of forgiveness for their failings and the failings will be many.

Even those who accept Christ are not going to get through this life perfectly, never 100% right. In fact some Christians fail so miserably that a "good life living" non-Christian lives a better life, a sad situation to be sure. Satan uses this phenomenon actively to convince many that God is unreasonable and unfair.

Truth is, God is both reasonable and fair. God gives us every possible opportunity to accept Him but in the lives of many Satan does prevent the salvation experience to the end. But since God is always beckoning us to come to Him the thought eternally in our mind will always be "Is this God thing real; should I buy-in; and accept God's plan as the Bible teaches?"

Why is it that this Christian versus non-Christian issue exists? Because we each are flawed, believer and non-believer, Satan's influence in this world will take its toll on our Christian potential; even as believers no matter how hard we try to be totally and completely "in Christ" at all times we fail and sometimes miserably.

In the flesh we sin. We read in 1 John 1:8:

> "If we claim to be without sin, we deceive ourselves and the truth is not in us." (NIV)

With the above logic I am not "going easy" on a Christian's need to maintain a serious and continual attempt to live a perfect life for Jesus. A word of caution is appropriate here.

There is one problem that can come psychologically when we Christians consciously work at and try very hard to be "perfect." Sometimes if we are not very careful, Satan will use this effort and try to convince us that we have gained with our own effort a certain "piety." Self-conceived piety yields pride, which causes us to engage in a "spiritual" look down on our fellow man. This is patently wrong for God says; "he

who is without sin cast the first stone." In every case the stones stay as they lay.
So as we strive for perfection we must always remember to "Love our neighbor as ourselves" as the second part of the greatest commandment.

Since Christians and non-Christians do sin it is for this cause that Jesus came to earth, to bring grace. In a Christian's life, if sin increases, then grace increases as stated in Romans 5:20b. "...but where sin increased, grace abounded all the more..."

This is absolutely true, unless we are playing games with God. However, grace will not increase if we continue sinning with the thought that, "Why not, doesn't God forgive sin?"

This "grace" came from and through the LOVE of God in the form of Jesus Christ to His created beings.

That's all of us, folks! May all claim God's way.

God Loves

To understand this concept of "God loves and cares" I believe we must -
---Free our minds of misconceptions about God!
---To do this we need to do the following:

We need to remember -

1. God created man. We are His workmanship!
2. That God did not create man to have someone to punish!
3. Rather God created man so that God would have someone to love and charged Man to love his Creator.
4. And finally God loves us more than we can imagine!

Just as the universe is unfathomable in size so God's love is unfathomable! God's love is so great that God's love purifies us (makes us righteous) even in our sin through believing in Jesus Christ! Read the Prophet Isaiah in foretelling the advent of Jesus some 700 years prior to His arrival -

> Isaiah 1:18 "Come now, let us reason together," says the LORD. "Though your sins are like scarlet, they shall be as white as snow; though they are red as crimson, they shall be like wool. (NIV)

More Love Scripture

We have looked at what Moses recorded from God, what Isaiah prophesied and what Jesus said about love. In the NIV "love" is used 319 times in the Old Testament and 232 times in the New Testament. What other scripture might help our study about the love of God? We find the Apostle John speaking about the love of God in his epistle 1 John 3:1 -

> 1 John 3:1 Behold, what manner of love the Father hath bestowed upon us, that we should be called

> the sons of God: therefore the world knows us not, because it knew him not. (KJV)

Here John is trying to portray to us the awesome nature of God's initiative toward us when He uses the term "what manner of love." John is calling attention to what God has given to us through Jesus. God actually makes each believer a full member of God's own family. Some refer to this as "the family of God." Peter refers to the family of God in -

> 1 Peter 4:17 For it is time for judgment to begin with the family of God; and if it begins with us, what will the outcome be for those who do not obey the gospel of God?
> 18. And, "If it is hard for the righteous to be saved, what will become of the ungodly and the sinner?" (NIV)

Should we actually believe that faith in Christ inducts us into God's family? If we do not, we should, for we indeed are in God's family, for in the scripture believers are called "the sons of God." And a "son" is in the family! Look to the scripture for this fact to be revealed-

> Matthew 5:9 Blessed are the peacemakers, for they will be called <u>sons of God</u>. (NIV)

> Galatians 3:26 You are all <u>sons of God</u> through faith in Christ Jesus, (NIV)

> Galatians 4:6 Because you are sons, God sent the Spirit of his Son into our hearts, the Spirit who calls out, "Abba, Father." (NIV)

Hebrews, Chapter 2 states that both the Savior and the "saved" are in the same family.

> Hebrews 2:9 But we see Jesus, who was made a little lower than the angels, now crowned with glory and honor because he suffered death, so that by the grace of God he might taste death for everyone.
> 10. In bringing many sons to glory, it was fitting that God, for whom and through whom everything exists, should make the author of their salvation perfect through suffering.
> 11. Both the one who makes men holy and those who are made holy are of the same family. So Jesus is not ashamed to call them brothers. (NIV)

We as mere mortals can love our children so intensely; but we know that God's love far exceeds even the love a Mother and Father have for their children.

The Apostle John Describes God's Love

The Apostle John on God's love -

> 1 John 4:7 Dear friends, let us love one another, for love comes from God.
> 8) Everyone who loves has been born of God and knows God.
> 9) This is how God showed his love among us:
> He sent his one and only Son into the world that we might live through him.
> 10) This is love:
> not that we loved God,
> but that he loved us and

sent his Son as an atoning sacrifice for our sins.
11) Dear friends, since God so loved us, we also ought to love one another.
12) No one has ever seen God; but if we love one another, God lives in us and his love is made complete in us.
13) We know that we live in him and he in us, because he has given us of his Spirit.
14) And we have seen and testify that the Father has sent his Son to be the Savior of the world.
15) If anyone acknowledges that Jesus is the Son of God, God lives in him and he in God.
16) And so we know and rely on the love
God has for us.
God is love.
Whoever lives in love lives in God, and
God in him.
17) In this way,
love is made complete among us
so that we will have confidence on the day of judgment,
because in this world we are like him.
18) There is no fear in love.
But perfect love drives out fear,
because fear has to do with punishment.
The one who fears is not made perfect in love.
19) We love because he first loved us.
21) And he has given us this command:
Whoever loves God must also love his brother. (NIV)

This brotherly love comes when we are in Christ "if." "If" what? "If" we work at it real hard, because the natural me, yes, even the Christian natural me would be used by Satan to rob me, yes even steal from me, these remarkable fruit of the Spirit. Galatians 5:22-23

If Satan is successful at robbing us of the "first fruit love" he thereby robs us completely. At that point, we are Christians in spiritual poverty. It is most unfortunate but many so-called Christians have been so robbed.

Do not let Satan steal from us what God has promised. Satan and his spirits agree on this, I propose, after we profess Christ, "they say" – "let's do our best to keep these new believers from having joy.

CHAPTER 16

Follow God with All Your Heart

"...then the Lord your God will keep His covenant of love with you...."

In Deuteronomy Chapter 7 God told the Israelites:

> Deuteronomy 7:11 Therefore, take care to follow the commands, decrees and laws I give you today. 12) If you pay attention to these laws <u>and are careful to follow them</u>, then the LORD your God will keep his covenant of love with you, as he swore to your forefathers. (NIV)

If we "...are careful to follow..." "...God will keep His covenant of love..." All these words of God were addressed to the Israelites through Moses!

How then do they apply to the non-Israelite? We can go to Romans Chapter 10 to find the answer.

> Romans 10:1 Brothers, <u>my heart's desire</u> and prayer to God for the Israelites is that they may be saved. 2. For I can testify about them that they are zealous for God, but their zeal is not based on knowledge.

3. Since they did not know the righteousness that comes from God and sought to establish their own, they did not submit to God's righteousness.
4. Christ is the end of the law so that there may be righteousness for everyone who believes. (NIV)

Romans 10:9 That if you confess with your mouth, "Jesus is Lord," and believe in your heart that God raised him from the dead, you will be saved.
10. For it is with your HEART that you believe and are justified, and it is with your mouth that you confess and are saved. (NIV)

God is at Work to Influence our Hearts

Remember God is at work in the lives of all people. Not only those who have said "Yes, to His wondrous plan for their lives by accepting His Son Jesus!" but, also "He is at work in the lives of those who have not yet decided to put their faith in Christ as Savior!" God and the Holy Spirit are continually at work, affecting the lives of the undecided, to continually place before them His desire for their hearts as well. Simultaneously Satan is trying to persuade us to either discount the plan of salvation or put odd our decision.

Romans 5:5 And hope does not disappoint us, because God has poured out his love into our hearts by the Holy Spirit, whom he has given us.
6) You see, at just the right time, when we were still powerless, Christ died for the ungodly.

> 7) Very rarely will anyone die for a righteous man, though for a good man someone might possibly dare to die.
> 8) But God demonstrates his own love for us in this: While we were still sinners, Christ died for us. (NIV)

God created life by "breathing into the created."

> Genesis 2:7 the LORD God formed the man from the dust of the ground and breathed into his nostrils the breath of life, and the man became a living being. (NIV)

As Creator He knows our very being! He knows our deepest needs! Since He created life He knows in infinite detail "just how" we can realize "love" in living!

How and why should we observe God's commands?

Many resist, asking what seems as a logical question. "If God created us to enjoy life why can we not direct our own lives and maximize our enjoyment in living on our own?

Why should I involve God?"

The first thing God tells us is to love Him.

He tells us to love "our GOD!"

We are first to love our Creator, then to love our neighbor as our self. To obey God, read our Maintenance Manual (the Bible) and seek His will and He will guide us in life's challenges. We find confirmation of this in the book of Proverbs.

> Proverbs 16:3 Commit your works to the LORD, and your plans will be established.
>
> Proverbs 16:9 The mind of man plans his way, but the LORD directs his steps. (NAS)

The above two verses tell us to "commit our works." To me these verses mean simply to remember that God enables us physically, and we are to commit our activities to God, and if we do this actively then God will assist in setting our life's plan in place and once that is complete God will "direct our steps" to insure the plans are accomplished.

If we stay tuned to His will and purpose. He will not, indeed cannot, direct our steps if we engage in any small way in a besetting and willful sinful pursuit; unless He attempts to guide us away from that sin.

CHAPTER 17

The Apostle Paul Defines Love

No scripture in the Bible defines love better or more completely than 1st Corinthians 13. This widely known chapter in the Bible is written using a series of statements that are "all encompassing" and uniquely define love.

Were there a contest from the work of writers down through the ages in defining a single word Paul would win easily for his definition of the word "love." Surely it would be hard to find a more masterful definition of any word. Paul did a wonderful job; I think through the hand of Paul writ God.

> 1st Corinthians 13 –
> If I speak in the tongues of men and of angels,
> but have not love,
> I am only a resounding gong or a clanging cymbal.
> If I have the gift of prophecy and
> can fathom all mysteries and
> all knowledge and
> if I have the faith that can move mountains,
> but have not love,

God's Love and Life's Polarities

I am nothing.
If I give all I possess to the poor, and
surrender my body to the flames,
but have not love,
I gain nothing.
Love is patient,
Love is kind.
It does not envy,
It does not boast.
It is not rude,
it is not self seeking,
it is not easily angered,
it keeps no record of wrongs.
Love does not delight in evil
but rejoices with truth.
It always protects,
always trusts,
always hopes,
always perseveres.
Love never fails.
But where there are prophecies,
they will cease;
where there are tongues,
they will be stilled;
where there is knowledge,
it will pass away.
For we know in part and
we prophesy in part,
but when perfection comes,
the imperfect disappears.
When I was a child,
I talked like a child,
I thought like a child,
I reasoned like a child.
When I became a man,

> I put childish ways behind me.
> Now we see but a poor reflection
> as in a mirror;
> then we shall see face to face.
> Now I know in part;
> then I shall know fully,
> as I am fully known.
> And now these three remain;
> faith,
> hope and
> love.
> But the greatest of these is Love.

I do not believe I need to explain what you have just read.

CHAPTER 18

The "Why" Question Answered

Open minded Scientists have concluded that when they run through all the scientific calculations related to nature's physical laws of the universe, one comes to a point where a very obvious concept appears irrefutable – an intelligent origin of the universe. One noted scientists in discussing this phenomenon said that at the end of the calculation one sees the "face of God." The nature of the complexity of the design of the universe points to the fact that the resulting conclusion is inescapable; that a master designer was at work when the creation event took place.

Then almost as amazing these scientists pose another question.

"Why?" Why did God create?

Could it have been, as postulated in 1st Corinthians Chapter One, for "heart love" to be experienced by God and man? I believe so.

As St. Paul posed in 1st Corinthians Chapter 11, of all human traits, "...the greatest of these is love!"

Why not love?

We can readily see from scripture God wanted love; indeed He "commanded love."

The evidence builds as Jesus spoke of God's desire for Man's love. Jesus condensed all the 10 Commandments to just two that He called the greatest commandment and it is all about "love."

> Mark 12:30 Love the Lord your God with all your heart and with all your soul and with all your mind and with all your strength.'
> 31 The second is this: 'Love your neighbor as yourself.' There is no commandment greater than these." NIV

Finally, I do not believe God's great LOVE can be expressed more poignantly and powerfully than in the hymn "Love is the Theme." Undoubtedly this hymn as written by an inspired hymnist expresses the reason for our earth and our very being as living "likenesses" of our Creator God.

Love is the Theme

Of the themes that men have known,
One supremely stands alone;
Through the ages it has shown,
'Tis His wonderful, wonderful love.

Refrain

Love is the theme, love is supreme;
Sweeter it grows, glory bestows;
Bright as the sun ever it glows!
Love is the theme, eternal theme!

Let the bells of Heaven ring,
Let the saints their tribute bring,
Let the world true praises sing
For His wonderful, wonderful love.

Refrain

Since the Lord my soul unbound,
I am telling all around
Pardon, peace and joy are found
In His wonderful, wonderful love.

Refrain

As of old when blind and lame
To the blessed Master came,
Sinners, call upon His Name,
Trust His wonderful, wonderful love.

Refrain

Yes, I believe God created for "love."

And if you accept His great love in Jesus Christ then this is not- "The End."

Rather it will be your eternal beginning.

www.ingramcontent.com/pod-product-compliance
Lightning Source LLC
LaVergne TN
LVHW011235080426
835509LV00005B/510
* 9 7 8 0 9 6 6 4 8 9 6 9 9 *